Publish and Flourish

A Guide for Writing in Education

Edited by

Bob Algozzine

Festus E. Obiakor

Jean N. Boston

Published by The Council for Exceptional Children

Library of Congress Cataloging-in Publication Data

Publish and flourish: a guide for writing in education / Bob Algozzine, Festus E. Obiakor and Jean N. Boston
    80 p.   Cm.
    Includes bibliographical references (p).
    ISBN 0-86586-319-9

A straight-forward look at critical aspects of scholarship in education. Writing journal articles, preparing grant proposals, publishing products, and other aspects of writing and continuing professional development are addressed by professionals with extensive relevant experience.

Stock No. P5273

Printed in the United States of America.
10 9 8 7 6 5 4 3 2 1

Table of Contents

Foreword

Reading *Publish and Flourish: A Guide for Writing in Education* was a pleasure. It is an assemblage of the craft knowledge of accomplished writers: useful, accurate, and level-headed advice for all education professionals interested in reaching colleagues by publishing their work. It also provides inspiration and motivation for the well-intentioned but unpublished among us.

Chapters in *Publish and Flourish* address publishing books, curricula, and other products; articles in both research and practitioner journals; and grant proposals. Potential audiences include graduate students, new faculty, and practitioners—but even experienced authors may benefit from the book's many useful features. The book is chockablock with tables, checklists, tip boxes, self-tests, and the like.

Publish and Flourish is not merely a how-to book. Chapters on the role of publication in professional development, the nature of scholarly discourse, and technology tools for writers were helpful and important extensions of its coverage. The chapter on minority scholars was a thoughtful addition as well. I also found the chapters with general suggestions for writers to be very helpful. Writing is difficult, and ideas about finding and using time, creating space, and identifying content and audiences are always welcome.

I think CEC members of all stripes will benefit from reading *Publish and Flourish*. It's the kind of book students, scholars, and product and curriculum developers need to have nearby—because they will refer to it frequently.

Paul Sindelar, Ph.D.
University of Florida

Preface

Publish and Flourish: A Guide for Writing in Education is written with the simple intention of encouraging more voices in general and special education. These voices are sometimes hidden or invisible because of the challenges associated with professional writing. For example, in higher education, coupled with teaching loads, professors are required to engage in other scholarly activities. This sometimes results in a competing relationship among teaching, research, and service. We appreciate the competitive aspects inherent in professional development. We also see a cooperative relationship among teaching, research, and service. Teachers have a lot to share through writing and researchers teach a lot with their writing, especially in the growth of their professions and knowledge within their fields. Both activities contribute to and benefit from professional service. This book resulted from years of experience engaged in and supporting professional development. We are convinced that the profession has more stories to tell and that these stories will continue to be hidden and invisible unless more of us tell them by overcoming the challenges of writing.

We had fun writing this book. It proactively addresses some of the "why" and "how" of telling stories in writing. To accomplish this, we invited individuals who understand the trials and tribulations of writing and frequently share their ideas. All of the chapters in this book show that writing can be challenging, but that it can also be rewarding. We believe the contributors of these chapters have answered many of the difficult questions about writing. It is our hope that this book presents a clear, proactive picture of the wonderful activity known as technical and professional writing.

Publish and Flourish: A Guide for Writing in Education is a book for new and seasoned writers. It is also a useful tool for undergraduate and graduate students. To be sure, doctoral students will find it very beneficial. Editors, mentors, scholars, researchers, and teachers can better help their students and each other by using this book in classes, presentations, and professional development. This book is for all those interested in unveiling their hidden voices through writing.

We thank The Council for Exceptional Children for its interest in the development of this book. We also express our gratitude to Anne Bauer, Anne Graves, and Paul Sindelar for their thoughtful reviews. Finally, we thank our families and colleagues for their unflinching support in this rewarding adventure.

Bob Algozzine
Festus E. Obiakor
Jean N. Boston

About the Contributors

Bob Algozzine, Ph.D., is a Professor in the Department of Educational Administration, Research, and Technology at the University of North Carolina at Charlotte. He has published more than 20 books and more than 200 articles addressing issues in assessment, evaluation, and teaching students with disabilities and learning problems. He has served as editor, associate editor, and field reviewer for numerous professional journals in general and special education and is currently the co-editor of *Exceptional Children*. He continues to mentor young and experienced scholars interested in highlighting their creative voices through writing.

Bob Audette, Ph.D., is an Associate Professor in the Department of Reading and Elementary Education at the University of North Carolina at Charlotte. He has been a school district and state department administrator with extensive experience producing, managing, and disseminating local, state, and national funded projects. He has written widely on quality principles in education and is currently investigating the efficacy of Total Quality Education in a large school district setting. He has served as a reviewer for a variety of general and special education journals, including most recently, *Action in Teacher Education, TEACHING Exceptional Children,* and *Exceptional Children.*

Anne M. Bauer, Ed.D., is a Professor of Early Childhood and Special Education in the Division of Teacher Education at the University of Cincinnati, Ohio. She is the author of 14 books and several chapters on classroom management and early childhood special education. She has served on many editorial boards including Behavioral Disorders and Remedial and Special Education. Currently, she serves as co-editor of *Teacher Education and Special Education*, The Council for Exceptional Children's division publication of teacher educators.

Jean N. Boston is the Senior Director of Continuing Education and Publications for The Council for Exceptional Children (CEC), Reston, Virginia. She has worked for CEC since 1972. For a number of years, she served as Associate Director for Publications and Marketing for the ERIC Clearinghouse on Disabilities and Gifted Education. Under her leadership, CEC has built a profitable book publishing program with a primary focus on meeting the needs of special education practitioners. Over the years she has brought more than 200 titles to publication, including books, audio tapes, videotapes, filmstrips, and digests. She also oversees the production of CEC's professional journals, *Exceptional Children* and *TEACHING Exceptional Children*. She continues to mentor educators, scholars, and professionals interested in marketing their innovative ideas.

Dave L. Edyburn, Ph.D., is an Associate Professor in the Department of Exceptional Education at the University of Wisconsin-Milwaukee. He is the author of the book, *The Electronic Scholar: Enhancing Research Productivity with Technology* (1999,

Merrill/Prentice Hall) and numerous book chapters and journal articles on the use of technology to enhance teaching and learning. He serves as a reviewer for several journals including *TEACHING Exceptional Children* for which he is the editor. In his capacity as editor, he mentors educators and scholars interested in writing practitioner-based articles.

Bridgie Alexis Ford, Ph.D., is a Professor of Education and Co-ordinator of Special Education in the Department of Counseling and Special Education at The University of Akron, Ohio. She is the author, co-author, or co-editor of several historic works related to the general and special education of African-American learners (e.g., the October/November 1992 special issue of *Exceptional Children* and *Effective Educator of African-American Exceptional Learners: New Perspectives*, published in 1995 by Pro-Ed). She serves as a field reviewer for *Urban Education* and editor of *Multiple Voices*, the publication of the Division for Culturally and Linguistically Diverse Exceptional Learners (DDEL), a division of The Council for Exceptional Children.

Mark B. Goor, Ph.D., is Assistant Dean of Academic and Student Affairs in the Graduate School of Education, George Mason University, Fairfax, Virginia. He is author and co-author of over 20 articles and chapters focusing on general and special education. He is the author and co-author of two books—his latest book, *Create More Time to Teach* is published by Sopris West. He reviews manuscripts for many scholarly journals and serves as associate editor of *Intervention in School and Clinic and Multiple Voices.*

Shariba Rivers Kyles is the Executive Assistant to the Provost at Medgar Evers College of The City University of New York in Brooklyn, New York. She is also a doctoral candidate (Higher Education Administration) at Louisiana State University, Baton Rouge, Louisiana. She has co-authored four book chapters and one review essay, and she currently serves as the editorial assistant for *New Frontiers in Urban Education*, a book series published by Corwin Press.

Kofi Lomotey, Ph.D., is the Provost and Senior Vice President and Professor of Education at Medgar Evers College of The City University of New York in Brooklyn, New York. He is the editor, co-editor, or author of six books and has published numerous articles and book chapters. His latest book, *Sailing Against the Wind: African-Americans* and *Women in U.S. Education,* was published in collaboration with graduate students he has mentored. Currently, he serves as editor of *Urban Education* and *New Frontiers in Urban Education*, a book series published by Corwin Press.

Teresa Mehring, Ph.D., is the Dean of The Teachers College and Professor of Psychology and Special Education at Emporia State University in Kansas. She has over 40 publications including books, assessment instruments, book chapters, and refereed journal articles. She is the author (in collaboration with Festus E. Obiakor and John O. Schwenn) of the 1997 book, *Disruption, Disaster, and Death: Helping Students Deal with Crises* published by The Council for Exceptional Children. She has more than 20 grants funded by state and federal agencies and private foundations. She is on the editorial board of *Intervention in School and Clinic* and reviews for many publishing companies.

Festus E. Obiakor, Ph.D., is a Professor of Special Education and Coordinator of the Graduate Mental Retardation Program in the Division of Psychology and Special Education, Emporia State University, Kansas. He is a teacher-scholar who has written more than 100 academic publications including books, chapters, monographs, articles, commentaries, essays, and poetry. In October/November 1992, he was the lead editor of the special issue of *Exceptional Children* and in 1995 he was a co-author of the book, *Effective Education of African-American Exceptional Learners: New Perspectives* published by Pro-Ed. Both landmark works addressed issues in the education of African-American youth in special education settings. He is on the editorial board of many scholarly journals including *Exceptional Children* and *Multiple Voices* for which he serves as associate editor. He continues to mentor writers interested in unveiling their hidden "multiple" voices.

James R. Patton, Ed.D., is the Executive Editor of Pro-Ed Publishing Company, Austin, Texas and an Adjunct Associate Professor in the Department of Special Education at the University of Texas at Austin. In his role as Executive Editor, he is in charge of the Books and Materials Division (i.e., the acquisition and development of quality products) and negotiates contracts with potential authors. He is the author of many books, chapters, and articles, and he continues to serve as an editorial board member of many scholarly journals.

Robert Rueda, Ph.D., is a Professor and former Chair in the Division of Learning and Instruction at the University of Southern California (USC). He has published widely in the areas of general and special education, psychology, and bilingualism. His most current work is funded by the OERI Center on Research on Education, Diversity, and Excellence (CREDE) at the University of California at Santa Cruz and also through the Mellon Foundation. He serves on the editorial board of several professional journals including *Exceptional Children* for which he served as the first associate editor from a minority background.

John O. Schwenn, Ph.D., is the Vice President for Academic Affairs and Professor of Special Education in the Division of Psychology and Special Education at Emporia State University, Kansas. He has over 40 publications including the co-authoring of eight books—he is the co-author of the book, *More Time to Teach*. He has written and obtained grants for many innovative programs such as Project Partnership at Emporia State University. He serves on the editorial board of numerous journals including *Multiple Voices* and *Exceptional Children*. Currently, he

is the editor of *Emporia State Research Studies*, a refereed publication that encourages faculty research productivity.

Fred Spooner, Ph.D., is an Associate Professor in the Department of Counseling, Special Education, and Child Development, University of North Carolina at Charlotte. From 1987-1996, he served as co-editor of *TEACHING Exceptional Children (TEC)*. In his capacity as co-editor, he mentored writers interested in publishing works that are practitioner friendly. He has co-authored numerous books, chapters, and articles on distance learning and general and special education issues. He is currently a reviewer for many scholarly journals including *Teacher Education and Special Education* for which he serves as associate editor.

Martha Thurlow, Ph.D, is an Associate Director of the National Center on Educational Outcomes and Research Associate in the Department of Educational Psychology at the University of Minnesota. She has published numerous books, articles, and training materials for use by professionals in general and special education and school psychology. She has served as editor, associate editor, and field reviewer for a variety of scholarly journals and is currently the co-editor of *Exceptional Children*. In her capacity as co-editor, she continues to mentor persons interested in publishing their qualitative and quantitative works in *Exceptional Children*.

Kenneth A. Weaver, Ph.D., is a Professor of Psychology and Chair of the Division of Psychology and Special Education at Emporia State University, Kansas. He has authored 40 articles, chapters, and books and reviews for many journals and publishing companies. One of his articles was published in *LIBRES: Library and Information Science Research Electronic Journal*, available only on the Internet. His new book, *Viva la Difference in Statistics*, published by Kendall/Hunt, includes computer data analysis.

Chapter 1

Catching the Writing Bug

Festus E. Obiakor, Bob Algozzine, and Jean N. Boston

Revelation

We make ourselves a place apart
Behind light words that tease and flout,
But oh, the agitated heart
Till someone really finds us out.

'Tis pity if the case require
(Or so we say) that in the end
We speak the literal to inspire
The understanding of a friend.

But so with all, from babes that play
At hide-and-seek to God afar,
So all who hide too well away
Must speak and tell us where they are.

—Robert Frost

Robert Frost's poem, "Revelation" (Lathem, 1969, p. 19) challenges our agitated hearts to reveal themselves. We all have had the urge to reveal our intentions on various issues in some form or fashion. Scholars, educators, and students always have had good ideas, but the worry is why, how, or where they should share those ideas. In respective communities, great orators and storytellers are consistently misrepresented as their stories pass from person to person. In other words, our stories are told unidimensionally when we only use speech to reveal our hearts' agitations. Spooner, Algozzine, Thurlow, Obiakor, and Heller (1997) noted that "no amount of discourse or rhetoric can remediate the inconsistencies in our history, values, and stories unless we write them down" (p. 19).

The urge to tell stories through writing is an intriguing phenomenon. Busy schedules with frequent daily demands weaken the urge and the action. We make excuses even when we have wonderful ideas to share. Henson (1995) wrote:

> Whether or not you are aware of your strengths, all workers perform some parts of their jobs exceptionally well. This means that you have information that is valuable to others who hold similar positions. But, month after month and year after year, aspiring writers attend writing workshops and openly acknowledge that they do not believe they have anything worthy of publication. This conclusion is unwise and it is wrong. You do have knowledge that is worth sharing, and until you acknowledge this truth you will remain unduly handicapped. (p. 29)

It is common knowledge that some issues and/or topics are more close to people's hearts. Since their likes and dislikes as human beings motivate them to attach different values to things, they can contribute to debates on those issues through writing. We are convinced that people can catch the writing bug; however, the critical issue continues to be why or how they spend their writing time. Our reactions to the possibilities are the major thrusts of this chapter.

Why Catch the Writing Bug?

Professionals who spend their time teaching and learning with others constantly have the urge to tell stories and share experiences. They also understand that these experiences will be inconsistently interpreted unless they share them in writing. To better understand these behaviors, consider some reasons for catching the writing bug.

Write to be Empowered

Writing is empowering. Self-knowledge and self-esteem are important variables; however, self-ideal is built through self-empowerment (Obiakor, Stile, & Muller, 1994). To be self-empowered, people must be cognizant of current issues confronting them. Many professionals try to share ideas at professional conferences often discovering great networking milieus that assist in disseminating ideas. Unfortunately, these same people sometimes become "gun-shy" when it comes to writing. Henson (1995) identified six personal myths that haunt potential writers. They are:

1. I'm not sure I have what it takes.
2. I don't have time to write.

3. I don't have anything worth writing about.
4. The editors will reject my manuscript because my name is not familiar to them.
5. My vocabulary and writing skills are too limited.
6. In my field there are few opportunities to publish.

The above myths are very dangerous because of their ramifications on personal self-worth. It does not take much to have an idea to share with colleagues—the only difference this time is that these ideas are to be shared in writing. *For instance, we had ideas for a book of this nature, we decided to share them in writing, and we involved colleagues who were also willing to share their ideas in writing.* These myths are also nonproductive alibis. The truth is that all of us make time for whatever we like to do. In addition, we all try our best in whatever we feel motivated to do. Our hunch is that writing is no different.

While some colleagues have had the urge to tell their stories, some have told us that they do not write because there is nothing new to write about. Some even challenge the quality of books and articles published by others. But, as the adage goes, "one person's junk is another person's treasure." Our experiences and ideas in this chapter might not make sense to one reader but they might be very valuable to other people. Henson (1995) indicated that "some people enjoy just sitting around talking about writing, telling why they don't write for publication . . . Others talk a lot about writing they plan to do, but they never get around to it" (p. 2). He added that "the world is full of people who dream about becoming something they aren't but who haven't the initiative to become whatever they wish to become" (p. 3).

Write to Manifest Energies of Freedom

To manifest our energies of freedom through writing, most people must go beyond the usual talk to action. Some years ago, Lorch (1981) explained that "the process of writing involves bringing together three separate and distinct elements and establishing relationships between and among them" (p. 32). These triangular elements are (a) the writer, (b) the reader, and (c) the subject matter. Bridges and Lunsford (1984) confirmed:

1. That writing is a powerful means of learning. Through writing, the writer refines his/her thinking. He/she toys with ideas; ideas toy with him/her.
2. That writing is a recursive act that most often proceeds not smoothly but in fits and starts as the writer struggles to find meaning.
3. That writing must be marked by significance. Thus, the writer's task is to reveal his/her insight into a particular topic to the reader.
4. That form is a function of meaning. (p. v)

The positive energies all of us manifest as human beings are based on how we unmask ourselves. Many of us unmask ourselves through writing and in the process derive freedom. According to Henson (1995):

> You can decide what you want to write, when you want to write it, and even where you want to write. Authors can even choose their audiences. Writing offers opportunity to earn recognition. Few professionals enjoy more admiration than successful writers. Most people also know that writing offers authors an opportunity to apply their creative talents. When you write, you invent; and then you share your creation with as many others as possible. Our society places much value on creativity. (p. 3)

Write to be on the Cutting Edge of Issues

Writing helps many to be on the cutting edge of issues. Others bridge the gap between researchers and practitioners through writing. Additionally, in any field, practitioners have a lot to say and write about. Spooner and Heller (1993) remarked that "the lingering problem is the translation gap between the usual author (teacher educator) and the relevant audience (teacher), a gap between research and practice" (p. 47). The irony is that teachers are knowledgeable about what works in the classroom even though they are the target audience of most educational publications. Spooner and Heller emphasized that teachers "should publish because they have much to gain as both author and audience" (p. 47-48). Written documents help to bridge historical gaps. "Writing is the full manifestation of discourse" (Ricoeur, 1976, pp. 25-26). In addition, "when stories are passed orally from person to person their accuracy begins to dwindle, but when they are written, they endure the test of time" (Spooner et al., 1997, p. 18). Apparently, the past, present, and future practices are connected through written documents. Simply put, writing advances history, and history advances writing.

Write for Intrinsic and Extrinsic Rewards

In colleges and universities, the predominant debate is whether teaching, scholarship, or service should be given top priority in continuing, tenuring, promoting, and rewarding faculty. The debate usually focuses on what the mission of a college/university is or ought to be. The person most referenced in these campus debates is Dr. Ernest Boyer (the late President of the Carnegie Foundation for the Advancement of Teaching) who consistently challenged higher education to reconceptualize its definition of scholarship. Boyer (1994) wrote:

> I'm concerned that in recent years, higher education's historic commitment to service seems to have diminished. I'm troubled that many now view the campus as a place where professors get tenured and students get credentialed; the overall efforts of the academy are not considered to be at the vital center of the nation's work. And what I find disturbing is the growing feeling in this country that higher education is a private benefit, not a public good. (p. A48)

We have great respect for Dr. Boyer's work and comments. We, too, have great concern for where America's higher education is going. People need less confusion and more consistency. The antithesis, however, is that Dr. Boyer shared his ideas not only orally, but also in writing. He published many books, monographs, journal articles, and newsletter materials. In fact, in some quarters, he has been viewed as one of the renowned scholars of the 20th century. We suggest that people do what Dr. Boyer did. For example, if your creativity lies in teaching, share your creative ideas about teaching with colleagues in writing—people are always searching for innovative teaching strategies. We believe teaching, scholarly, and service activities go (and should go) hand-in-glove. They are not mutually exclusive, they are mutually inclusive. How can a teacher be a "great" teacher if he or she is not current in his or her field? Also, how can a teacher be a "great" teacher if his teachings are incorrect and archaic? The legitimacy of what is being taught is derived from current scholarship evaluated and authenticated by peers. Action, accountability, and achievement keep us current.

Writing has both intrinsic and extrinsic rewards. Personally, we are excited when we see our names in print and when our works are acknowledged or used by others. There is usually no end to this excitement, whether it is the first publication or not. That excitement, on its own merit, can be motivating and empowering. Through writing, we earn the respect of colleagues, students, and the professionals who interact with us. For example, our experiences have shown that students respect professors who use their published works as handouts for instruction. Additionally, professors earn tenure and promotion because of their scholarly contributions to the field. Spooner et al. (1997) reiterated:

> Many university programs survive because of the writing efforts of their faculties. Funded grant proposals and manuscripts published in professional journals provide evidence of successful writing efforts. Most proposals will not be funded unless they are well written and well targeted to address current problems. Some knowledge base and technical skills are required to produce a good grant proposal. Results of these grants are in turn published as books, book chapters, and research articles to increase visibility. (p. 19)

How to Catch the Writing Bug

All of us have something important to say; and because of it, we also have something important to write about. The critical question is, How do we go about writing? While there is no one model, there are specific styles (e.g., the American Psychological Association style) that writers must adhere to. The act and process of writing must be known and put into practice (see Tip 1.1). Lorch (1981) explained that "the act of writing is a process made up of understandable parts. It is not a mysterious flow of words from pens. An understandable process can be taught and learned. Everyone who writes effectively learned at one time how to do it" (p. 6). The process of writing involves (a) picking a topic that you think has potential and asking questions to generate information you may use in your writing, (b) sketching a tentative purpose and structure for your writing, (c) selecting and analyzing your audience, and (d) writing your draft in light of your purpose and choice of audience (Bridges & Lunsford, 1984; Obiakor, Lomotey, & Rueda, 1997).

Tip 1.1: Know your story and style. You need to know your topic or theme of interest and pursue it in detail. Not only must you know your topic, you must also know the act and process of writing (e.g., this process might be visible in the style that you choose to write your story—know the author guidelines of the publishing entity).

It is important to understand that you must proactively go after the writing bug in order to catch it. You must not be "gun-shy" about unmasking yourself through writing (see Tip 1.2). As Henson (1995) pointed out:

1. The competition among writers is keen. To succeed, writers must write excellently.
2. Good writers are self-made, not born. By learning a few hard facts, you can master the skills needed to succeed in writing.
3. Successful writing for nonfiction magazines, journals, and books requires above everything else—the ability to write clearly.
4. Plain, simple writing is preferred over sophisticated, esoteric, pompous writing.
5. Successful writers are organized. They have designated times and places for writing.
6. In our busy society, nobody makes or finds the time to write. Successful writers assign a higher priority to writing than to other activities.
7. Clear goals give writers direction and incentive.
8. Self-discipline and self-motivation characterize successful writers. You are the only one who can give yourself the kick in the pants that is needed to get started. (pp. 24-25)

Tip 1.2: Unmask yourself through writing. Enjoy your freedom and use your creative talents to create ideas. Do not be "gun-shy." You maximize your potential when you understand the connection between writing and freedom.

Writing involves hard-work and dedication. No writer writes perfectly the first time; however, it helps to view writing as an attitude not as a job. It becomes a stressor when we view it as a compulsory job— it loses its fun. Spooner and Heller (1993) stated that "a 25-page paper of publishable quality does not automatically or easily appear on the page because one wishes it to be there" (p. 48). In writing, you can be your own worst enemy. Many people talk about publishing in what they call the "top journal"—we all have friends like them (see Tip 1.3). In reality, procrastination and ego are counterproductive to writing. As Spooner and Heller contended, to write productively, we must (a) be at our physical best, (b) manage our writing environment, (c) keep track of our ideas, (d) let our ideas flow, (e) use an outline, and (f) write the first draft.

Tip 1.3: Talk less and write more. Let your writing do the talking. Avoid the "victim" mentality and empower yourself through writing. Set your priorities straight. Do not make writing your stressor. Have fun!

Through the years, we all have mentored many people in writing. We have discovered that many professionals put off writing until they want to get either tenure or promotion. The fact remains that people grow in writing by writing—there is no magic formula that will solve all writing problems. Writers just need to write, sometimes with others as we have done in this chapter (see Tip 1.4). To become a better writer (a) study a topic intensively, (b) confront challenging and important issues, (c) conduct systematic work with colleagues, (d) write clearly and with style, (e) embrace feedback, and (f) do not lose perspective (Algozzine, Obiakor, & Spooner, 1997; Kiewra, 1994; Obiakor et al., 1997).

Tip 1.4: Collaborate with colleagues in your writing. Involve people in your writing projects because "two heads are better than one." Colleagues might add new perspectives to your thinking. By writing with other people, you advance the context of history, and the context of history advances you.

Perspective

We are all agitated hearts who have something to say or share. Why and how we should share our ideas continues to interest and intrigue us. We argue in this chapter that if people respond to agitations through speech alone, their stories will be told unidimensionally. We also suggest that no amount of rhetoric can remediate the inconsistencies in our stories unless we write them down. We are not born writers—we learn to write by writing.

Our experiences tell us that anybody can catch the writing bug. Positive thinking is an important key. The time spent "talking big" or "knocking down" other people's works could be spent on productive writing activities. Planning is also important—writing does not do itself; it is a skill that requires hard work and dedication. Yet, it should not be viewed as a stressful job. Most of us cannot afford to put off writing until it is time for tenure or promotion. When we do this, we become our own worst enemies. While there is no one formula for writing, you can do some things to make your writing better. Henson (1993) suggested that we (a) write captivating titles, (b) use subheadings to capture attention, (c) write fluidly, (d) write simply, (e) write assertively, and (f) show application. We must try to know our audience, the readers. In addition, it pays to write with others— they add multiple voices. We conclude with the words of Lewis and Sugai (1996), "before you sit down to write, identify one or two important points you would like to make, who your audience will be, and what information the reader will need to replicate your idea or critically analyze your point" (p. 16). The points we tried to make here are: (1) There are many reasons to catch the writing bug and all of them are important to professional educators and (2) there are many ways to catch the writing bug and all of them are within the reach of all professional educators. We leave the making of other points to the writers who follow us in this book.

References

Algozzine, B., Obiakor, F. E., & Spooner, F. (1997, April). *Writing for publication.* Paper presented at The Council for Exceptional Children Annual International Convention, Salt Lake City, UT.

Boyer, E. L. (1994, March 9). Creating the new American college. *The Chronicle of Higher Education, p. A48.*

Bridges, C. W., & Lunsford, R. F. (1984). *Writing: Discovering form and meaning.* Belmont, CA: Wadsworth.

Henson, K. T. (1993). Six ways to capture and hold the attention of nonfiction readers. *Writers' Journal, 14,* 19-20.

Henson, K. T. (1995). *The art of writing for publication.* Needham Heights: Allyn and Bacon.

Kiewra, K. A. (1994). A slice of advice. *Educational Researcher, 23,* 31-33.

Lathem, E. C. (Ed.) (1969). *The poetry of Robert Frost.* New York: Holt, Rinehart and Winston.

Lewis, T. J., & Sugai, G. M. (1996, Fall). A guide to preparing manuscripts for publication. *Beyond Behavior, 7,* 16-17.

Lorch, S. (1981). *Basic writing: A practical approach.* Cambridge, MA: Winthrop.

Obiakor, F. E., Lomotey, K., & Rueda, R. (1997, January). *Writing for publication.* Paper presented at the Multicultural Symposium of the Division for Culturally and Linguistically Diverse Exceptional Learners (DDEL), The Council for Exceptional Children, New Orleans, LA.

Obiakor, F. E., Stile, S. W., & Muller, D. (1994). Self-concept in school programs: Conceptual and research foundations. In F. E. Obiakor & S. W. Stile (Eds.), *Self-concepts of exceptional learners: Current perspectives for educators* (pp. 1-18). Dubuque, IA: Kendall/Hunt.

Ricoeur, P. (1976). *Interpretation theory: Discourse and the surplus of meaning.* Fort Worth: The Texas Christian University Press.

Spooner, F., Algozzine, B., Thurlow, M. L., Obiakor, F. E., & Heller, H. W. (1997). Ethnic minority scholars writing for professional publication: From myth to reality. *Multiple Voices, 2,* 12-20.

Spooner, F., & Heller, H. W. (1993). Writing for publication in journals for practitioners: Suggestions for teachers and early career researchers. *Remedial and Special Education, 14*(3), 47-52.

Chapter 2

Professional Development Means Being Known for What You Do

Bob Algozzine, Fred Spooner, and Anne M. Bauer

I was brought up to believe that the only thing worth doing was to add to the sum of accurate information in the world.

—Margaret Mead

In practically every institution of higher education there are explicit or implied policies and procedures that assist and, perhaps, even direct the process of professional development of individual faculty in departments and colleges. So that a coherent message is being broadcast to faculty about acceptable professional behavior and what related contingencies of promotion and tenure entail, department and college policies are usually in line with expectations at the university level. In some of these documents, there may be general statements of broad expectations such as supporting the mission and programs of the college appropriate to one's role, demonstrating integrity and high standards of ethical and professional behavior, and *being* collegial, collaborative, human, and respectful of diversity. At a more precise level, there are likely to be statements which facilitate the definition of teaching, service, and research activities that help shape and direct all professional development activities.

For most faculty in higher education, teaching is the basis for their employment. It typically involves such activities as providing content area instruction, advising students, and supervising practical classroom experiences as well as student-directed scholarship. Professional development in teaching is usually supported by supplying a statement about one's teaching philosophy, demonstrating expertise and currency in the content area of one's assigned courses, incorporating instructional technology into teaching, and evaluating instruction via peer and student evaluation.

Applying knowledge in one's field beyond the university classroom provides opportunities for professional development. Generally, these service activities occur in three domains:

- Service to the profession (e.g., roles in governance of professional state and national association such as The Council for Exceptional Children [CEC] or one of its divisions; serving on the editorial board of a professional journal such as *Teacher Education and Special Education*, the journal of the Teacher Education Division [TED] of CEC;
- Service to practitioners and community (e.g., local CEC chapters and local schools);
- Service to the institution such as serving on departmental committees (e.g., search committees for new positions), college committees (e.g., tenure and promotion committees), university-wide committees (e.g., committee on distance learning).

Evidence to evaluate service is typically represented by some of the following activities: sustained involvement in professional organizations and associations in one's field at state, re-

gional, national, and international levels, contributions to professional organizations or associations that are focused and that draw upon one's professional expertise; and leadership in addressing important issues relevant to one's profession.

Research usually means expanding the knowledge base in one's field (e.g., severe disabilities, behavior disorders, and mild mental retardation) with scholarship and professional writing that synthesize and integrate extant information or disseminate the results of experimental or quasi-experimental studies. Evidence to support research activity is usually provided by a clearly articulated research agenda and focus; a documentation of collaboration with colleagues, including junior faculty, in efforts to expand the knowledge in their respective fields; and a sustained record of scholarship and professional writing reflecting systematic efforts to conduct, report, and disseminate empirical research.

Most new and experienced faculty have little trouble compiling teaching and service records that are valued by their university peers. Typically, teaching assignments are distributed systematically to faculty with expertise in program areas. Similarly, service opportunities are everywhere. The area that presents more concern and less certainty is research. Too often, faculty are provided little guidance in designing a research agenda, developing collaborative relations, and meeting reasonable publication standards. On the other hand, research is often the most potent variable in the professional development equation, and levels of anxiety rise disproportionately with levels of uncertainty associated with scholarship, professional writing, and research.

In this chapter, we focus on two areas that we believe support professional development productivity. First, we illustrate the importance of integrating teaching, service, and research activities. Then, we provide some guidelines that maximize efforts in scholarship and professional writing.

Integration Is Key to Success

Many who have been successful in higher education are those who have found a way to integrate their teaching, research, and service, so that these activities are not totally discrete and unrelated experiences. Those individuals who excel are those who have been able to find and establish an integrated focus for their respective professional careers. The people who are successful are those who usually have a relatively clear idea about how to make their research, teaching, and service support one another. At a basic level, an individual with doctoral level training, let's say in the subdiscipline of severe disabilities, would more than likely teach courses in the area of severe disabilities and wouldn't teach courses in the area of the gifted. A person with expertise in the area of severe disabilities would likely belong to professional organizations such as CEC's division on Mental Retardation and Developmental Disabilities (CEC-MRDD) and The Association for Persons with Severe Handicaps (TASH). From a teacher education perspective, that same individual might also belong to CEC's Teacher Education Division (TED). This professional would likely try to "carve-out" his or her specialty niche in professional associations, seek to participate not only in their annual meetings as a way to present research findings, but likely also entertain the idea of serving on various committees within these organizations as a way to, in part, engage in relevant service as part of career development activities. The research agenda for this individual could proceed in one of a number of different directions which relate to persons with severe disabilities.

The research paradigm (e.g., qualitative or quantitative) that one adopts is, in part, to some significant degree, based on what one studies, and the research tools that were likely used to complete one's dissertation (e.g., single subject design vs. a groups approach). Although most researchers typically know one of the research paradigms very well, they shouldn't rule out the possibility of expanding their ability to approach a research question. Let the question at hand, in part, dictate which type of research method that best addresses the question under investigation. In many cases, working with other colleagues, those who are "like minded," and perhaps, some who pursue research from different perspectives, will help to expand one's knowledge about research designs. Often times, if a research question is carefully phrased, and the study precisely articulated, the experimental outcomes under analysis will yield insight for the next experimental investigation (Johnston & Pennypacker, 1980). Maybe there isn't an individual who is interested in your research question, per se, but someone may be interested in assisting with designing the next study, with a particular set of analyses in mind. In most instances, working together with a team of persons maximizes the effort. Members of the team can decide their respective roles in the current investigation or multiple investigations who will do what and when (e.g., who will take the lead on which manuscripts, who will write conference proposals to be submitted for potential presentations, and which organizations the research group will target for the next academic year). Perhaps, there are individuals with whom you went to school who are now employed at different spots around the country who have similar programmatic and research interests as you. Just because you are no longer located at the same physical location does not preclude the opportunity to collaborate. It may make it somewhat more difficult, but with e-mail and the capability to send totally intact attached documents from one location to another, collaborating with a colleague from another university, even if it is three time zones away, or halfway around the world, is becoming easier than ever before in history. As your professional career develops, you may even cultivate collegial relationships with individuals whom you meet at association meetings. You attended their presentation at a conference, and made a judgment that they do good work, not only that they do good work, but are interested in the same topic. You make arrangements to speak with them, a research agenda is crafted, roles and responsibilities are delineated, and a partnership is forged.

Being able to conduct, report, and disseminate research is an important component of a productive professional development portfolio. A good rule of thumb to follow in academia is: Think twice about the activity that is pursued, and if you can't write about it, present it, or make it fit into the rest of your professional expectations, think twice about whether it is really worth doing. Each component of a professional development portfolio of research, teaching, and service should complement each other. Decisions about how you spend your time as a professor need to be carefully crafted, so that each piece fits together as part of the whole. You must always consider how these parts fit together. How can service complement research? How can research enhance teaching? And, always, ALWAYS, you must take into account how the activities in which you engage can be documented, how each integrates with the larger picture, and above all, how, if you do it, you can write about it: Does what you are doing have the potential to become a manuscript or product that can be used as evidence of professional productivity?

Scholarship and professional writing are, in many cases, the most important part of a faculty member's tenure and promotion dossier because publications are widely respected as evidence of advancement of knowledge. Members of the respective departmental review committees are, usually, knowledgeable of the important journals in one's discipline, and such contributions can be evaluated (quantitatively and qualitatively). A quick review of publications and articles in press can readily reveal gaps in a candidate's writing record, or trends that expose periods of relative inactivity, followed by bursts of attempts at writing as a mandated review approaches or balance in published material over the long haul. Although teaching and service are complementary components to one's professional career, this is academia, not a position in public service nor is it a teaching role at a local community college, and scholarship, professional writing, and the generation of new knowledge are highly valued.

For many underrepresented faculty groups (e.g., women and minorities) who lack strong support bases, the pragmatic response to the question, "Why publish?" could simply be to remain employed. Besides this practical response, Hardin (1991) and Hartman (1991) concurred that women need to research and publish to generate new ways of knowing and thinking. For instance, women faculty may not be taken seriously nor respected for their contributions to the field without publication. As Obiakor and Ford ask in Chapter 3 of this book, "Who will tell your stories correctly in writing if you do not?" Women need, and have, justifiable grounds for claims to tell fewer false stories about gender, social relations, nature, and reality. For these related reasons, women and other underrepresented faculty groups should view scholarship as an imperative phenomenon.

Making the Most of Your Scholarship and Professional Writing

If a report is to be submitted or a manuscript is to be published, it must first be written. Words, phrases, sentences, paragraphs, and sections of a written product just do not magically appear on the page, as if they were written by a "Writing Assistant." Usually trying to find the time to write does not produce manuscripts either. Writing takes discipline.

For most faculty in higher education there are many competing priorities in one's professional life, let alone those things in one's personal life that also compete for time in one's daily schedule. From a professional perspective, there are lectures to prepare, classes to teach, students to advise, papers to grade, phone messages to which one needs to respond, and now in the age of more frequent electronic communication, e-mail messages, some of which are more pertinent than others, that also require a response. With all of these activities, and perhaps even others, how does one find the time to write? We could say that it is really quite straight-forward, one simply MUST MAKE THE TIME! Writing takes discipline. This call for discipline on time management takes an interesting turn for women in higher education considering their traditional values of taking care of everyone in the family.

Those in higher education who have not only survived, but actually flourished under the publishing contingencies of academia have somehow found a way. Although there are probably some similarities to many of the success stories that you are likely to hear from your colleagues about how they get it done, the formula is based on individual need—different strokes for different folks. Consider a few examples. Everybody has a colleague (Dr. X) who thrives on 11th hour, "crash and burn" activities. Dr. X always manages to "get the job done," but there is always plenty of doubt in the minds of those with whom Dr. X works. Dr. X's opposite-end-of-the-continuum colleague (Dr. C) systematically steps from the beginning to the end of a project with the precision and timing of a well-executed symphony. Dr. C has a place for everything and the only problem is deciding what project to do first. Similarly, some folks are morning people, and others tend to do their best work at the opposite end of the clock. Some find that their office at the university, after the bulk of the regular workday is completed, meetings are finished, and most of their colleagues have gone home, is the place where they write. Others work at home where they have a professional space, perhaps even an office that has all of the comforts of a well-designed work area, better than the one provided by the university.

There is no magic in successful writing. The key is maximizing effort, which is not a new idea (c.f. Skinner, 1981; Spooner, Algozzine, Thurlow, Obiakor, & Heller, 1997; Spooner & Heller, 1993). The spin put on it in this chapter is grounded in the work of Skinner (1981) and supports five maxims: (1) Put yourself in the best place for writing, (2) Take advantage of technology, but don't be controlled by it, (3) Stay away from connected prose as long as possible, (4) Model the successful behavior of others, and (5) Don't give up on failure or rest on success.

Put Yourself in the Best Place for Writing

First, a little exercise, adequate rest, and an appropriate diet can't hurt. We usually do not do our best work when we are tired, either mentally, physically, or both. A daily schedule that includes some time away from writing, the amount of sleep that is appropriate for you, a little nourishment to refuel the system, and some type of exercise can go a long way to freshening your perspective on professional tasks. Next in that daily schedule, you must make some time for writing. As discussed earlier, morning, afternoon, evening, or after midnight, it doesn't matter, as long as it works for you. It is a good idea to let your output help you evaluate what times work best (see Tip 2.1).

Once you have established a place and a time to write, you can practice in the location that you have just identified. You must take time to arrange your books and your professional journals, get the appropriate files on the hard drive of your computer, and make sure that information is backed up daily. There will be occasions when you are away from your desk and you get an idea about the piece that you are currently developing. Ideas need time to percolate.

> *Tip 2.1: Identify a writing lifestyle that works for you.* Much like you might do a budget when thinking about what to do with your money, make some systematic decisions about what to do with your time. This means making decisions about personal as well as professional time. A familiar adage begins "all work and no play..." and it should ring true in planning your writing lifestyle.

Stay Out of Prose as Long as Possible

Writing is thinking written down. The essence of writing is rewriting. The essence of rewriting is thinking about writing. Writing is a continuous process. All writing begins with a "blank sheet." For many, the most difficult stage of writing is producing the first complete, cogent sentence. Fear of failure, perils of perfectionism, and paralysis by analysis make many reluctant to put those first words on paper. Remember, writing is thinking written down. To facilitate the transition from thoughts to written products, it helps to keep track of ideas that come to you when you are not at your desk but still thinking about writing. Your "brainstorms" may come when you are driving in the car to your university location, they may come as you are walking to class, and they may even come as you are setting the table for dinner, or at some other, seemingly, odd time. You must create a mechanism to capture those ideas, jot them down on a scrap of paper, or have an official "list of notes." The notes do not have to be the beginning of a formal document. They are just notes, written in some hieroglyphic that perhaps only you understand. The important thing is that you have written enough, and made it legible enough, that when you look at what you have written, at some later point in time, you can capture or recapture the essence of what you have written.

At this point, the ideas should trigger phrases, the phrases sentences, the sentences paragraphs, and the paragraphs products. The form and shape may follow a typical "research" article with the standard sections of abstract, introduction, method, results, and discussion as its components or become the filler for an outline (Fuchs & Fuchs, 1993). It is a good idea to take the writing task one component at a time. Assuming that the data are already analyzed and you are well aware of the outcomes, begin to jot down information for the introductory section, taking into account the three or four major studies that have laid the groundwork for the current piece of research. It is now a matter of highlighting the salient pieces of those studies and delineating how your work stems from them. Get the points down first, go back later, and build in the transitions, from one paragraph to the next, from one study to the next. There may be additional ideas that come to you that could potentially fit in the discussion section; keep track of those on your note pad.

As the points appear, you should begin to see how one point relates to the next, and how the points relate to the whole. At this stage a final product begins to develop. As with the notes, nothing formal is in order. You must check to see if what you have written relates one point to the next, and then see if all of the necessary points are included. After you have written a chapter or manuscript, list the title, headings, and subheadings on a separate sheet of paper exactly as they appear in the body of the text. You can use this "reverse outline" to check to be sure that similar level headings reflect similar levels of content importance.

Writing is thinking written down, putting thoughts on paper, rewriting, and thinking about what you have written (see Tip 2.2). Avoid fears of failure, perils of perfectionism, and paralysis by analysis: Just write and rewrite until you get it right!

Tip 2.2: Think of all your writing as a work in progress. Don't spend too much time writing the perfect title, sentence, paragraph, page, or document. Work from ideas that you accumulate on paper. Take those ideas that are accruing and begin to develop them into a product. When the product is done, review it to be sure it presents the message you wanted.

Take Advantage of Technology But Don't be Controlled by It

RAM, DRAM, Thank you, madam! Technology is changing our lives. Routine writing tasks like outlining, editing, and revising take less time today, and they are simply easier than ever before in history. Paradigm shifts occur in the field of technology every 18 months; important changes occur more frequently. To keep up, you must go with the flow. Do not use an out-of-date application if a greatly improved, more powerful one comes along. You must be prepared to "upgrade" to improve your writing lifestyle and an overall productivity shift will happen.

Many faculty members at any college or university were "paper trained;" that is, they were taught to write using a pencil and paper, and then expected to give their work to someone else to type. Or, they often prepared a handwritten draft of a document or portions of a document and then typed it themselves. Think of all the extra effort expended! For all practical purposes, they were doing the work twice (i.e., writing it down, and then typing it). In the age of information technology and personal computers, this would appear to be a sound and prudent

decision. If you do not have a computer, get one. If you do not already know how, learn to type and compose at the keyboard. If you still need the paper to be more productive, do your editing and rewriting on printed copies of your work.

Of course, writing involves more than putting the fingers to the keyboard and sending some form of coherent visual output to a screen. It also means reviewing what has been written, reading material that relates to what you are writing, and maybe even taking a trip to the library, if necessary, to locate additional resources. On any writing project, it makes sense to include time away from the machine. Remember, it is a machine and you should control what it does (see Tip 2.3).

Tip 2.3: Use technologies to improve your writing. The Internet is a powerful writing resource. In addition to searching for information on specific topics and educational journals, there are dozens of Web sites where you can find self-help information on writing. Here are just a few: On-line Resources for Writers: http://webster.comment.edu/writing/writing .htm; Writer's Workshop: http://www.english.uiuc.edu/ cws/wworkshop/ww_hand.html; and Elements of Style: http://www.cc.columbia.edu/acis/bartleby/strunk/.

Model Successful Behavior of Others

If you are writing a manuscript for publication in a professional journal, check recent issues for author guidelines or obtain a copy directly from the editor or publisher. While they may not be very specific about what will be published, they typically offer broad advice regarding content and style that can be very helpful in preparing your work. They also provide the correct name(s) and address(es) to guide the submission process. It is also a good idea to find two or three written products that you like and use them as models for your own work. What you write should be your own words, but reviewing recent issues of the journal you are considering as a publication source for something you have written can be very helpful in putting it all together.

While it is generally considered more acceptable in the tenure and promotion stream to have published in notable refereed journals in your field, you should not avoid other sources. The more you write, the better you will be at writing, and a written product is better than no product at all. Small subscription journals that are highly focused in content coverage can be excellent sources for something you have written. Similarly, the reviews you might receive from such a submission can go a long way in helping you improve your work for another journal. If you are just beginning a writing career, it is usually a good idea to begin with "less powerful" journals because it might be frustrating to begin with a tough journal like *Exceptional Children* or a similar journal focused heavily on research and characterized by a high rejection rate (see Tip 2.4). It is a good idea to contact editors to find out information about acceptance rates, special issues, or turnaround time if you cannot find it in the journal. The more information you have about what has been published (i.e., successful models), the better prepared you will be to write a successful publication (Henson, 1997).

Tip 2.4: Set goals you can easily achieve. Nothing breeds failure like failure and nothing breeds success like success. Holding yourself to standards that are too high is a sure way to become an unsuccessful writer. Productive faculty engaged in teaching, service, and research typically publish 3 to 5 articles a year (some years more and some years less). Be reasonable, don't plan more than you can accomplish, but be sure you accomplish something and be proud of what you have done.

Don't Give Up on Failure or Rest on Success

Writing is hard work and nothing makes hard work harder than failure. If something you write fails to be accepted, you must not give up on it. Successful writers respond favorably to rejection. They view it as an opportunity to improve what they have written. The essence of writing is rewriting. You must not get trapped by failures or successes in writing (see Tip 2.5). For women and other underrepresented faculty groups in higher education, their foci could be participatory and dialogic forms of writing if those are where their strengths lie. Do not give up! To avoid the "giving up" behavior you must use your intuition, collaborate, find a mentor, form or join a writing group, and find out "what counts" and do it. For instance, if chapters do not support your attainment of tenure or promotion, explore other forms of publication. Nevertheless, you must find your voice, your style, and your genre.

Tip 2.5: Build on success, don't rest on it. Even if something you have written is accepted without revisions, look for ways to extend, augment, and improve its message. Consider everything you have written a work in progress. Let your colleagues review your work and offer suggestions on how to improve it, even after it is published.

Perspective

Sometimes you will write to give something back to your profession. Sometimes you will write to attempt to improve your profession. Sometimes you will write to improve your teaching. Sometimes you will write to advance your career. Whatever the reason, you can always improve your writing. Here are a few of life's little instructions to help along the way.

- Dream big dreams, but be known by what you write; written products are better than ideas regardless of why you produce them.
- Small works done are better than great works promised and undone; even the longest novel was written one word, sentence, paragraph, and page at a time.
- Spend time fixing problems rather than fixing blame; there are plenty of reasons for not writing. Avoid them like the plague.
- Do not separate who you are from what you write—by maintaining who you are, your contributions become unique.
- Unveil your hidden voices through writing.
- Avoid accepting assignments that won't be finished; nothing breeds accomplishment, confidence, and satisfaction like achievement and success.

- If you are not having fun writing, try writing something that is fun; commit yourself to quality, but remember, there is a game to be played here.

Personal Perspective on Writing

One thing we have learned after many years working and writing together, the adage "different strokes for different folks" rings true when trying to pinpoint productive strategies of successful writers. To provide some indication of what works for at least one of us, we provide a brief case study illustration of a day in the life of a productive publishing professional.

Mornings at home surpass other times and locations as the best "place" for writing. Although airline travel (e.g., writing on airplanes en route to a conference presentation) can be somewhat conducive to writing (i.e., no phones to answer, no students to advise, and you really don't have to carry on much of a conversation with the person in the seat next to you), there is simply more room at home to create a lifestyle that works. Daily output can be printed to see how products composed at the keyboard look on paper. It is also easier to complete a daily writing session and then intersperse some time away from writing to take a break (e.g., go for a run) and think about what has been written (e.g., think about the big picture and how the most recent writing fits, develop new ideas that relate to the points being made in a paper, and prepare a mental outline). Typically, 2 or 3 hours a day are spent on writing projects before putting them away for the rest of the day. After going to the office, professional activities (e.g., committee meetings, responding to professional correspondence, and voice mail and e-mail, advising students, and preparing for class) other than writing take precedence, but there are plenty of opportunities to jot down thoughts and mental notes for the next day's writing. Classes scheduled in the late afternoon or evening make the morning writing lifestyle work well.

References

Fuchs, L., & Fuchs, D. (1993). Writing research reports for publication: Recommendations for new authors. *Remedial and Special Education, 14,* 39-46.

Hardin, S. (1991). Who knows? Identities and feminist epistemology. In J. E. Hartman & E. Messer-Davidow (Eds.), *(En)gendering knowledge: Feminists in academe* (pp. 100-115). Knoxville, TN: The University of Tennessee Press.

Hartman, J. E. (1991). Telling stories: The construction of women's agency. In J. E. Hartman & Messer-Davidow (Eds.), *(En)gendering knowledge: Feminists in academe* (pp. 11-34). Knoxville, TN: The University of Tennessee Press.

Henson, K. T. (1997). Writing for publication: Some perennial mistakes. *Phi Delta Kappan, 78,* 781-784.

Skinner, B. F. (1981). How to discover what you have to say: A talk to students. *The Behavior Analyst, 4,* 1-8.

Spooner, F., Algozzine, B., Thurlow, M. L., Obiakor, F. E., & Heller, H. W. (1997). Ethnic minority scholars writing for professional publication: From myth to reality. *Multiple Voices, 2,* 12-20.

Spooner, F., & Heller, H. W. (1993). Writing for publication in journals for practitioners: Suggestions for teachers and early career researchers. *Remedial and Special Education, 14*(3), 47-52.

Chapter 3

Expressing Diverse, Minority Scholar Voices

Festus E. Obiakor and Bridgie Alexis Ford

Black at Last

Closely did I sit with my forefathers
Who patiently sacrificed for my freedom;
The coconut juice melted
like ice as it dripped slowly into my mouth;
The highway to the Egyptian Pyramid
seemed out of reach as I trekked
in the midst of the dreaded Crab-Bucket Syndrome;
Nearly did I hide my Blackness,
And, nearly did I hide my Brilliance;
My energy came back slowly and surely
as I continued my journey;
The distance got shorter and the sight of those
bamboo roofs reminded me of the Pyramid's creativity;
Black at last I was
as I touched the Egyptian Pyramid
built with Brilliance and Strength;
And I promised my forefathers,
Never again, and never again
will I hide my Blackness, Brilliance, and Beauty.

—*Festus E. Obiakor*

In this poem, Obiakor (1998) highlights the beauty and brilliance of "Blackness," and acknowledges the perseverance, determination, and energy needed to succeed in one's endeavors. In some fashion, he asks, "What would have happened had the creators of the Egyptian Pyramid discontinued their creative venture because of their predicaments (e.g., the hotness of the weather)?" "Where will our freedoms be today had our forebears given up due to hardships of slavery and domination?" Throughout history, no freedom has ever been free; it results from commitment and sacrifice.

Traditionally, books, monographs, journal and newspaper articles, and testing instruments have failed to reflect cultural and historical values of ethnic minority members. There have been several complaints, and some minority group members have tried to set the records straight through writing. Sometimes, these efforts have not been respected or rewarded by colleagues, and to a large extent, many important historical facts continue to be missed in the literature. To this end, we ask one simple but critical question. Who will tell your stories correctly in writing if you do not? Based on this question, it is imperative that minority scholars write not only for professional reasons but also for self-pride. This is the major premise in this chapter. In addition, we share our experiences and provide tips for success in expressing diverse scholarly voices.

Reasons to Publish: Minority Scholar Perspectives

There are many reasons to publish; however, for ethnic minority scholars, the objectives are twofold: (a) to create truths and respond to inaccuracies, and (b) to advance career opportunities through self-determination. Responding to each enhances productivity for all.

Creating Truths and Responding to Inaccuracies

A scholar can be regarded as a seeker of truth. For those in special education, this process often entails redefining and creating paradigms to positively address multidimensional issues that confront children and youth from culturally and linguistically diverse backgrounds and their families. The importance of researching and disseminating accurate information through publishing is clear (i.e., to address overall problems in special education and recommend solutions). The historic and continued negative treatment given to ethnic minority learners by general and special education systems makes the distribution of accurate information imperative (Ford, Obiakor, & Patton, 1995). The thorough examination of issues surrounding effective educational service delivery for ethnic minority populations has been traditionally ignored, perceived as irrelevant, or addressed negatively by some non-ethnic minority scholars (Littleton, 1995). It appears that biased and inaccurate research findings have dominated major journals in education. Unfortunately, these findings influence educational policies (e.g., federal level decision making and practices Littleton, 1995).

There has been a recent increase on multiculturally related issues in major special education journals and periodicals. This, in turn, has increased the visibility of many ethnic minority scholars who focus their works on alternative paradigms and practices for culturally diverse children and youth with disabilities and/or gifts and talents. In spite of this visibility, systematic permeation has not occurred. We are strongly convinced that until ethnic minority scholars deal with issues surrounding quality service delivery to ethnic minority youth and their families, minority perspectives will remain controllably invisible in significant journals. In addition, the "truth" should not be limited to a few privileged ethnic minority scholars and special multicultural themes and issues. Ethnic minority scholars must take advantage of new outlets and challenge existing paradigms through writing.

Granting agencies are another force that can contribute to the presence of ethnic minority scholars in major journals. Research conducted through funding helps to provide the content for redefining and creating novel paradigms and practices. As a result, ethnic minority scholars must write grant proposals that focus on culturally and linguistically diverse children and youth with disabilities and/or gifts and talents. The results of these grant projects can lead to the dissemination of needed information to promote more positive student outcomes. For some ethnic minority scholars, publishing represents the traditional value of giving back and elevating the community, in particular its youth—the future generation. Concomitant with creating appropriate alternative models, ethnic minority scholars have the challenge of rebutting biased and inaccurate research about ethnic minority populations. In other words, ethnic minority scholars have to operate from both offensive and defensive perspectives (e.g., creating, redefining, and rebutting inaccuracies) by focusing on "what is and what is not" (Hine, 1996; Hooks & West, 1991; Littleton, 1995). Littleton noted that defensive publishing consumes a large amount of time, yet it must be done but not at the expense of creating and defining positive appropriate models and practices to influence service delivery for multicultural learners. For minority scholars, balance is a key to enhanced performance.

Advancing Career Opportunities Through Self-Determination

Professionals in higher education are well-acquainted with publish or perish policies. Publishing plays a decisive role in hiring, promoting, and tenure processes (Phillips, 1993). Where the work is published is important; works published in major journals are generally awarded more credit (Garrett & McLoughlin, 1995). The publishing process can present difficulties to many faculty members in colleges and universities. Some of these difficulties can be particularly painful for new ethnic minority faculty trying to adjust to their environmental milieu. When difficulties are externally induced (e.g., trying to urge minority scholars to select nonmulticulturally related research themes in order to be accepted and promoted), the individual scholar, the

special education field, and more importantly, exceptional children and youth from culturally and linguistically diverse backgrounds become losers. On the other hand, when difficulties are self-induced (e.g., fear of rejection of manuscripts), everyone loses. Factors that serve to promote an increase in ethnic minority scholars' publishing in major journals include (a) receptive editorial boards, (b) adequate representation of ethnic minority scholars on editorial boards, (c) peer reviewers who possess appropriate levels of awareness and knowledge in multicultural issues, (d) sufficient time to think and write, (e) supportive mentoring systems, and (f) productive professionals providing a continuing stream of quality scholarship (Hooks & West, 1991; Littleton, 1995; Spooner, Algozzine, Thurlow, Obiakor, & Heller, 1997).

Institutions of higher learning, like the society in which they exist, can sometimes be less receptive of issues related to cultural and linguistic differences. This lack of attention can manifest itself in low student-ratings of minority faculty and staff in teaching and stereotypic regard for scholarship and service. Bell (1985, 1992) highlighted many of these racially unjustified activities. As a result, the only redemption for an ethnic minority professor is to write. Furthermore, writing acts as both therapy and opportunity opener. If the teaching load is heavy and much time is spent serving on committees as a minority figurehead, professional advancement will be very difficult.

Ethnic minority professors must be careful not to allow themselves to be set up for failure since writing is a big part of professional development and advancement. Even when they know they are being used by their institution, they need to be preparing themselves at all times for advancement and movement. Writing provides them with this freedom to have opportunities and make choices. Henson (1995) put it succinctly:

Writing is an empowering activity. Many individuals enjoy the power they derive from writing and the power derived from subsequent publications. For example, professors enjoy the respect that they get from colleagues and students when their articles and books are used in classes . . . Perhaps the most meaningful empowerment is internal. Having a manuscript accepted for publication is evidence of your power; just knowing that your article has been approved by a national panel of experts in your field reassures you that you are on the cutting edge. (pp. 3-4)

Lessons from Experience: Beyond Myths

Multicultural special education is a renewed phenomenon, and there is a dearth of works in this important area of education. Gollnick and Chinn (1990) confirmed that "throughout U.S. history, racial identification has been used by policy makers and much of the population to classify groups of people as inferior or superior to another racial group" (p. 85). This historical misclassification has led to racial stereotypes, labels, discrimination, exclusion, and illusionary conclusions. Today, because of this historical misclassification, scholars and educators of culturally and linguistically diverse backgrounds are forced to remain vigilant in their search for and dissemination of the "truth." As a result, voices that have been invisible in the literature are becoming not only visible but also multiple. Obiakor (1994) and Peterson (1991) agreed that this enthusiasm has elevated multi culturalism as an inevitable force worthy of complementing major theoretical frameworks such as humanism, behaviorism, and cognitive learning theory. In addition, this enthusiasm has produced scholarly writings that have attempted to equalize the negative effects of historical writings. Unfortunately, the real impact of such scholarly efforts is yet to be felt in special education. For children and youth with exceptionalities (and their families), the limited inclusion of research and writings by minority scholars remains problematic. In addition, ethnic minority scholars have been somehow ineffective in dealing with traditional exclusionary practices in their scholarly writings. For instance, deciding not to write because of rejection or other exclusionary policies appears counterproductive and self-defeating. This decision, in our opinion, is like accepting defeat before the war even begins.

To fully discuss divergent perspectives about writing in scholarly publications, we share the experiences we have garnered from our writing activities. These perspectives are based on (a) historical burdens of exclusion, (b) The Council for Exceptional Children's (CEC) current efforts, (c) mentoring opportunities, (d) editorial experiences, (e) avoidance attitudes, and (f) constraints of time and location. These perspectives are addressed in the following subsections.

Historical Burdens of Exclusion

There are historical burdens that ethnic minorities continue to endure in mainstream society. These encumbrances have far-reaching effects on how minorities view opportunities and choices in education (Obiakor, 1993). Ford, Bessent-Byrd, and Misaka (1997) presented a paper entitled, "Contributions of Culturally and Linguistically Diverse Ethnic Groups to Changing Paradigms in Special Education," at CEC's 1997 International Convention. This presentation celebrated CEC's 75th anniversary and showcased the varied roles of ethnic minority professionals through the years. In preparing for their presentation, Ford and her associates researched written records and consulted with several elders in the field to clarify and validate their findings. In terms of scholarly publications, their investigation concluded that ethnic minority professional writings were limited in special education journals and other publications. They did, however, discover a few Multicultural Proceedings, sporadic issues of major CEC journals, and a couple of books targeted to address ethnic minority issues in special education. Additionally, they found inconsistent inclusion of writings by ethnic minority scholars within the major CEC journals about issues regarding culturally diverse individuals with disabilities and/or gifts and talents.

Historically, culturally focused research and topics addressed by many ethnic minority scholars tend not to receive the same high level of acceptance as legitimate and quality research as nonculturally oriented topics (Ford et al., 1997; Hine, 1996; Hooks & West, 1991; Littleton, 1995; Spooner et al., 1997). Even the most privileged and prolific ethnic minority "elder" and "more recent" scholars have their stories of frustration regarding acceptance and publishing of their work. Of course, frus-

tration with the publication process is not the exclusive domain of minority scholars. In this regard, two critical questions deserve some attention: Must one prove his or her scholarship and acceptance by writing about general problems without focusing on issues having the most impact on youth from culturally diverse backgrounds and their families? Must one's work on any topic be written in a conservative, status quo tone to be accepted by the editorial board of major journals?

The review process for publication typically uses a blind review of peer experts to evaluate the quality of the work (Garrett & McLoughlin, 1995). An essential concern within this process is reviewers' expertise on cultural and linguistic diversity issues. The literature continues to reveal the inadequate preparation of special education personnel to provide effective services for children and youth from culturally and linguistically diverse backgrounds (Ford et al., 1995). Several factors contribute to this issue, one being the lack of expertise by teacher educators themselves. Teacher educators comprise the largest percentage of most expert peer reviewers. Though these peer reviewers may be experts in special education, they may not be knowledgeable about genuine multicultural special education issues. Interestingly, the argument of reviewer expertise also recently surfaced when "qualitative" researchers perceived their work as less likely to be published in "quantitative" journals.

While this decade has witnessed some increase in ethnic minority scholars' presence as editorial board members or guest reviewers of major special education journals, this representation remains limited. An argument often used in defense of limited acceptance of ethnic minority works within prestigious publications is that alternate culturally oriented publication outlets are available for these scholars (Phillips, 1993). This line of argument appears enticing, but it shifts responsibility and limits the literary mechanisms available to put forth research findings that can be used to influence policy decision making. Another issue surrounding peer expertise that needs attention is the valuing of the expertise of ethnic minority scholars as peer reviewers. For example, although we have been involved in many projects as reviewers, we have sometimes been asked in a rather belittling manner, to defend our expertise. We do not feel that other leaders in the field of special education are forced to authenticate their expertise the way ethnic minority scholars are implicitly forced to do.

To really reduce these inconsistencies and the historical burdens of exclusion, it is imperative that ethnic minorities think about writing as a contribution to history (see Tip 3.1).

> *Tip 3.1: Think about writing to create truths and reduce inconsistencies.* Write to contribute to the future and to overcome the historical burdens of exclusion that sometimes characterized the past.

CEC's Current Efforts

Of late, there have been current efforts by CEC to be inclusive at all levels. CEC recognizes that for inclusion to be successful, there must be inclusion at the classroom, school, and community levels. More minority scholars than before are on editorial boards of major CEC journals. Representatives of these major journals have consistently held national workshops to encourage ethnic minority professionals to publish. Unfortunately, very few ethnic minority persons take advantage of these sessions. At its annual convention CEC has supported more strand presentations of serious thinking and scholarship on multicultural special education. In addition, there have been multicultural summits to have a meeting of the minds and reveal critical issues facing multicultural persons in special education. These issues tend to be old and new and highlight topics that attract major publication outlets.

The establishment of the Division for Culturally and Linguistically Diverse Exceptional Learners (DDEL) by CEC a few years ago provided an added boost in bringing to the forefront issues related to multicultural special education. DDEL publishes *Multiple Voices for Ethnically Diverse Exceptional Learners (Multiple Voices)*, a refereed journal that addresses paradigms, research, policies, and daily school practices to reduce inequities in educational opportunities for culturally and linguistically diverse individuals with disabilities and/or gifts and talents. In *Multiple Voices* both authors of this chapter serve as Associate Editor and Editor respectively, and more than 85% of its editorial board members and guest reviewers are minority group members. At CEC's national level, there is more networking among ethnic minority scholars. This networking milieu has provided mentoring opportunities for neophytes in the scholarly arena—some scholarly publications have resulted from these endeavors (see Tip 3.2). Two questions continue to be critical at this juncture. How can ethnic minority members maximize the benefits of CEC's efforts? Similarly, how can CEC maximize talents of its ethnic minority members?

> *Tip 3.2: Take advantage of CEC's current efforts.* These efforts include summits and symposia that highlight topics that attract major publication outlets. Put together a manuscript or series of papers and actively seek publication sources. If the past has been unkind, let the future be better.

Mentoring Opportunities

Experiences in mentoring ethnic minority scholars and educators tell us that writing myths can be debunked. We agree with Henson's (1995) notion that "good writers are self-made, not born" (p. 24). We also agree that "barriers that impede the success of ethnic minority faculty in professional writing can be overcome" (Spooner et al., 1997, p. 14). Mentoring and networking provide ample opportunities for writing impediments to be removed. Obiakor (1997) observed that such a networking milieu provides multidimensional opportunities for experienced ethnic minority scholars to mentor inexperienced ones. Many of the myths associated with scholarly writing could be easily addressed with appropriate mentoring, collaboration, and partnership.

Mentoring fails when collaboration, cooperation, and consultation fail. Not long ago, Henson (1995) confirmed that "when personalities are compatible, collaborating can bring out the best in all. Each partner stimulates the other. The unique expertise of each writer complements that of the others. For academics who are required to publish, collaborating can accelerate the role of publishing of all partners" (p. 129). Collaboration and partnership in this instance mean shared responsibility toward mutual goals—they do not mean having another person do a greater portion of the job. They mean taking pride in your work through continuous communication as professionals. Obviously, people cannot collaborate when one is the "victim" and the other is the "victimizer" or when one is the "victim" and the other is the "savior." To this effect, ethnic minority scholars must take advantage of mentoring opportunities (see Tip 3.3). They must also understand very early that whatever they put out is a reflection of them whether they like it or not (Obiakor, Lomotey, & Rueda, 1997).

> *Tip 3.3: Discover a writing mentor.* As a mentee, demonstrate the willingness to learn. Do not be a victim or a victimizer. Contribute first with ideas and later with actions. Learn quickly and try to give more than you take.

Editorial Experiences

Our experiences in serving as editorial board members of many scholarly journals have revealed that writing myths deserve debunking (Henson, 1995; Spooner et al., 1997). Henson identified these myths to include statements such as (a) I'm not sure I have what it takes, (b) I don't have time to write, (c) the editors will reject my manuscript because my name is not familiar to them, and (d) in my field there are few opportunities to publish. Spooner and his associates noted that "these myths can be dangerous to writers from ethnic minority backgrounds because they have broad self-concept and productivity implications. Writing is hard work, and perceptions that detract from our willingness to do it just make it more difficult" (p. 14).

We believe in the old saying, "it ain't over 'til it's over." Our experiences have shown that many ethnic minority writers take rejection too literally—they internalize rejection instead of looking at it as a way to better their works. Our own success in scholarly writing is based on our willingness to revise and resubmit our manuscripts. We acknowledge that race, color, and tribalization matter in all societal activities in the United States (Obiakor, 1994; West, 1993); however, negative presumptions about publications pose serious challenges for ethnic minority scholars. These presumptions tend to perpetuate the "victim" mentality which in itself hampers scholarly production and increases the blindness on human differences. We cannot in good faith deny the tremendous support that many of our nonminority colleagues have given to us. Our experiences have also revealed that many of these same individuals are quite knowledgeable on issues related to culturally and linguistically diverse exceptional learners.

As a consequence, we cannot assume that all editorial rejections are based on racism or discrimination. A rejected article might be a good article that needs to be revised and resubmitted to either the same publication or another publication (see Tip 3.4). The presumption that you have to know somebody to publish is wrong. Rather, when you write consistently, you are known. Consider this analogy. When a business produces quality products, many customers buy from it and it becomes popular and widely known. Before long, this business builds its own clientele and makes more profit than its competitors. A consistent writer is no different. When you do quality work, people will respect and reference it in their own works even when they disagree with you. Before long, you gain a credible national and international reputation, begin to serve on editorial boards of publications, and enjoy invitations to submit your works for publications in myriad outlets.

> *Tip 3.4: Do not take editorial rejection too literally.* Take advantage of free advice often provided in manuscript reviews. Revise and resubmit rejected manuscripts to the same source or other publication outlets.

Avoidance Attitudes

When we think about our pains, trials, and tribulations in writing, avoidance sometimes crosses our minds. Out question continutes to be: If we do not write, who will rectify the historical falsities and inconsistencies in the educational literature? This is a serious challenge to ethnic minority scholars. Our experiences have revealed that avoidance attitudes create more problems and more stereotypes for ethnic minority members in the scholarly arena. We must be consistent and persistent in telling our stories in writing in spite of our frustrations (see Tip 3.5). Spooner and his associates (1997) wrote:

1. Since we all have stories to tell, we all have what it takes to be good writers. We must be self-motivated and self-empowered to write.

2. We make time for whatever we like to do. We cannot dismiss the inconsistencies in our history unless we make time to write.

3. There are many issues confronting us. These issues are worth writing about.

4. Everyone's manuscript can be rejected. No one is immune from rejection. Rejection of a person's manuscript does not in any way mean rejection of that person.

5. We improve our vocabulary and writing skills by writing. Remember, writers are self-made, not born.

6. There are many opportunities for people from diverse cultural and linguistic backgrounds. Today, almost all professional conferences and publications focus on issues facing these groups. Since our demographics are changing, these issues cannot be swept under the rug.

7. We must enjoy the power that writing brings. To decry tokenism, we must enjoy the power associated with publication of books, monographs, articles, and other forms of writing. We cannot continue to be victims. We must define ourselves through our works.

8. We must collaborate, consult, and cooperate with people. Writing enhances teamwork and teamwork enhances writing. Individuals in different institu-

tions can have similar interests and different perspectives that enrich written products.

9. Our freedoms are incomplete unless we express them. An important medium for such expression is writing. (pp. 14-15).

> *Tip 3.5: Be consistent* Do not allow frustration to lead you into the avoidance attitude. Treat a letter of rejection as an opportunity to respond rather than a mandate to issue a death knell to a paper or as a reason to gripe and complain or become a victim.

Constraints of Time and Location

Lack of time and time management are frequently cited as primary stumbling blocks to publishing (Hine, 1996; Phillips, 1993; Spooner et al., 1997). Scholars in higher education have to acclimate themselves to the general barriers and stress of managing time to write. Common complaints include too many committees, large numbers of advisees, and heavy teaching loads. In addition to the demands expected of most professionals, many ethnic minority faculty and staff in predominately White colleges and universities are often pulled in several other directions. Some of these tasks include being called upon by departments to serve on committees needing departmental representation by ethnic minority faculty; serving as unofficial advisors, role models, and mentors for ethnic minority undergraduate and graduate students; and responding to demands for minority participation from church and other social or civic organizations within local communities (Hine, 1996; Phillips, 1993).

Nonethnic minority professionals adjusting to new geographic locations may also experience feelings of loneliness and isolation. However, for ethnic minorities, in particular females, these feelings may be more frustrating, especially in small predominantly White college towns (Hine, 1996). These feelings combined with other responsibilities (e.g., family, church) may limit energy and time for research and publishing. Thus, it becomes necessary to be aware of and embrace effective techniques to enhance collaboration and consultation in publishing. From our perspective, the best solution is to network, collaborate, and consult with other colleagues who have similar scholarly interests. Consistency in time management is the key (see Tip 3.6).

> *Tip 3.6: Manage your time.* If you are in any location, collaborate and consult with others of similar scholarly interests. Actively seek collegial relations; don't wait for them to knock on your door.

Tips for Success in Expressing Diverse Scholarly Voices

Ethnic minority scholars cannot afford to be silent, and our profession cannot afford to have their voices invisible. The reasons for them to write go beyond the usual writing for pleasure or promotion. As indicated, when ethnic minorities write, they create truths and respond to inaccuracies. From our personal perspectives, we enjoy the trials and tribulations of writing and we continue to learn a lot about writing by writing (see Tip 3.7). Based on our experiences, we strongly believe to maximize the potential for writing in scholarly publications, ethnic minorities must

1. Participate in workshops, seminars, and panels that lead to research opportunities.
2. Select an area of study that is personally or professionally meaningful and develop a research theme.
3. Present at national conferences and submit work to ERIC Clearinghouses.
4. Become a member of or create a network of publishing professionals.
5. Submit manuscripts to both traditional and culturally oriented special education publications.
6. Submit manuscripts to general and mainstream education journals and other publication outlets.
7. Write in order to learn how to write.
8. Reject historical burdens of exclusion that may wear them down.
9. Revise a rejected manuscript and resubmit it.
10. Ask to serve on editorial boards as they develop their craft.
11. Manage their time effectively.
12. Become a mentor and mentee depending on experience, expertise, and need.
13. Write some more even when they are known in the field—this is when their ideas might be getting the attention they deserve in the literature.
14. Be persistent and consistent about writing in scholarly publications.
15. Enjoy what they do.

Tip 3.7: Write, write, and write some more! Enjoy what you do; put your eyes on the prize; and add depth, perspective, and weight to multiple voices. Do not expect the world to provide a living. Look for opportunities and turn them into evidence of competence, credibility, and creation.

Perspective

In this chapter, we addressed reasons for ethnic minority voices to be heard in the literature. We used personal experiences to share our ideas about writing for publication without fear. Because we agree race, color, and tribalization continue to matter today in general and special education programs, ethnic minority scholars and educators have the obligation to debunk existing negative stereotypes that lead to illusionary conclusions. We understand barriers that hamper scholarly publications of ethnic minorities exist, but we also know from experience that these barriers can be overcome. To deal with them, we must understand the intricacies of writing for publication (e.g., to be a good writer, one must write). We cannot afford to be victims of our external or internal circumstances. We must tell our stories in writing to reduce historical inconsistencies in the literature. Through writing, we are bound to create truths, equalize negative historical writings, build scholarly reputations, and advance professionally. The solution is the same for everyone: Be known by what you do, not by reasons you can find to justify not performing.

References

Bell, D. (1985). *And we are not saved: The elusive quest for racial justice.* New York: Basic Books.

Bell, D. (1992). *Faces at the bottom of the well: The permanence of racism.* New York: Basic Books.

Ford, B. A., Bessent-Byrd, H., & Misaka, J. (1997, April). *Contributions of culturally and linguistically diverse ethnic groups to changing paradigms in special education.* Paper presented at the International Convention of The Council for Exceptional Children, Salt Lake City, UT

.Ford, B. A., Obiakor, F. E., & Patton, J. M. (1995). *Effective education of African American exceptional learners: New perspectives.* Austin, TX: Pro-Ed.

Garrett, J. E., & McLoughlin, J. A. (1995). A reference for judging the quality of publication in special education and related services journals. *Teacher Education and Special Education, 18,* 133-138.

Gollnick, D. M., & Chinn, P. C. (1990). *Multicultural education in a pluralistic society* (3rd ed.). New York: Merrill.

Henson, K. T. (1995). *The art of writing for publication.* Needham Heights, MA: Allyn and Bacon.

Hine, D. C. (1996). *Speak truth to power: Black professional class in United States history.* Brooklyn, NY: Carlson.

Hooks, B., & West, C. (1991). *Insurgent black intellectual life.* Boston, MA: South End Press.

Littleton, A. C. (1995). Research in education: Methodological and theoretical consideration. *Journal of Negro Education, 45,* 78-88.

Obiakor, F. E. (1993). Opportunity and choice in higher education: Perspectives of African American scholars. *SAEOPP Journal: Journal of the Southeastern Association of Educational Opportunity Program Personnel, 12,* 31-44.

Obiakor, F .E. (1994). *The eight-step multicultural approach: Learning and teaching with a smile.* Dubuque, IA: Kendall/Hunt.

Obiakor, F. E. (1997, Spring). Networking: African American dilemma. *Special Educators News and Update, 2,* 2-6.

Obiakor, F. E., Lomotey, K., & Rueda, R. (1997, January). *Writing for publication.* Paper presented at the Multicultural Symposium of the Division for Culturally and Linguistically Diverse Exceptional Learners (DDEL), The Council for Exceptional Children, New Orleans, LA.

Obiakor, F. E. (1998, January). *Black at last.* Emporia, KS: Emporia State University.

Pederson, P. B. (1991, September/October). Multiculturalism as a generic approach to counseling. *The Journal of Counseling and Development, 70,* 6-12.

Phillips, M. C. (1993). Tenure trap: Number of obstacles stand in way of tenure for women. *Black Issues in Higher Education, 21,* 42-43 & 45.

Spooner, F., Algozzine, B., Thurlow, M., Obiakor, F., & Heller, H. W. (1997). Ethnic minority scholars writing for professional publication: From myth to reality. *Multiple Voices, 2,* 12-20.

West, C. (1993). *Race matters.* New York: Vintage Books.

Chapter 4

Overcoming Challenges That Face New Writers

Mark B. Goor

They can because they think they can.

—*Virgil*

New faculty members often feel they have been "thrown to the wolves." Surveys of junior faculty (Hamilton, 1996; Renegar, 1993) reveal that most had no experience with publication during their doctoral programs to prepare them for this career requirement. These new faculty members imagined when they began their new profession there would be pressure to publish, but certainly there would be the time and support to succeed in this endeavor. Instead, new faculty members find themselves overwhelmed with teaching and institutional responsibilities (Boice, 1993) while realizing at the same time that senior faculty have little intention of being their mentors (Renegar, 1993). The same institutions that advertise positions for assistant professors with strong evidence of potential for scholarly achievement, essentially defined as successful publishing, make little or no provisions for providing the time or developing the necessary skills. The culture expects self-initiative and heroic dedication.

In spite of this lack of preparation and support, many new faculty members succeed as writers. What do these successful writers do? Successful writers confront their apprehension about writing and fear of rejection. They identify multiple sources of issues and select ideas they care about deeply. They make the time to write and push past the blocks to productiveness. They cultivate their creativity and demonstrate the willingness to contact editors and take criticism constructively. They enlist support of peers, senior faculty, and administrators. In addition, they edit their work ruthlessly and pay careful attention to guidelines and details of manuscript submission. Most of all, they enjoy the rewarding journey. To a large extent, this chapter addresses these areas and the following subsections discuss each in more detail.

Confronting Fears

To publish, new faculty members must confront writing anxiety. Most people have "writing apprehension" which centers primarily around locus of control (Rechtien & Dizinno, 1997). In other words, the degree to which writers feel they have control over their own success determines their relative anxiety with the process. Henson (1987) recalled that successful writers say "I can and will succeed," while unsuccessful writers are consumed by fear of rejection. Thus, as in most areas of competence and performance, attitude appears to distinguish successful from unsuccessful writers (See Tip 4.1). The successful writer has confidence and determination, and apprehension is diminished when enjoyment replaces anxiety related to writing.

Seeking Topics

Successful writers know the current issues because they read (Westermann, 1994), attend conferences (Henson, 1987) and collaborate with schools (Paul, Duchnowski, & Danforth, 1993). Good writers are good readers (Westermann, 1994). They ex-

> *Tip 4.1: Attitude is not everything, but it clearly matters in performing most skills.* Believing that writing is important, believing that competence in writing can be learned, and believing that you can write are convictions that shape powerful writers. Remember, attitude is one characteristic that distinguishes successful writers from unsuccessful writers.

plore many potential sources for publishing, obtaining a sense of each journal's topic areas, audiences, variations in style and formats, as well as the importance of research to each. Writers attend conferences to identify current topics and to create professional networks (Henson, 1987). Themes of presentations at these professional meetings provide insights into subjects of contemporary interest, and presenters often discuss their current research. If young writers have similar interests that have creative sparks ignited at a conference, they can talk to presenters about related research or writing ideas (See Tip 4.2).

Collaboration with schools provides a rich source of writing ideas. In a special issue of *Teacher Education and Special Education*, faculty members from the University of South Florida describe how a commitment to collaborate with schools is creating a new vision of teacher education and research (Paul, Duchnowski, & Danforth, 1993). Partnerships with educators and parents test educational theory, foster collaborative thinking, and stimulate new ideas for research and publication. In addition, many new faculty members have dissertation research data that can be translated into articles. It is best if this is done immediately as interest in dissertation topics often cools quickly.

> *Tip 4.2: Nobody knows everything and nothing lasts forever.* New ideas are everywhere. Find current topics by reading, attending conferences, and collaborating with other professionals.

Finding Passion

Reading, attending conferences, and collaborating may result in many ideas for publication, but it is vital to select a topic the writer cares about deeply (Clark, 1994). Westermann (1994) stated that authors should write about personal experiences that give power and color to their writing. Authors who participate and observe write with authenticity.

Writing can be hard work, and passion for the topic may be the only motivation that gets authors through difficult times (See Tip 4.3). Writers develop relationships with their topic and their manuscripts. As with all relationships, writers must learn to live through disappointments and frustrations by holding the vision for their work. Sometimes putting aside a project for awhile, or seeking guidance to move past perceived blocks, is just as necessary as getting space or counseling is to the health of a human relationship.

> Tip 4.3: One of the marks of productive writers is the ability to convert passion into action. An action becomes genuinely important when it springs from intrinsic motivation. Writing is hard work, and passion for the topic may be the only incentive that gets authors through difficult times.

Making Time

Top selling novelist Barbara Kingsolver contends there is no perfect time to write; there is only now (in Clark, 1994). Henson (1987) recognized that many authors work best at a certain time of day. Some write better first thing in the morning while others prefer late nights. Clark noted that artistic inspiration is overrated and recommended writing daily. If an author waits for the inspiration to write, the project may never get finished.

Successful writers do not *have* the time to write, they *make* the time to write, scheduling writing like they schedule teaching, meetings, and appointments (See Tip 4.4). Too often, when writing time is conceptualized as a few stolen moments to get as much done as possible, writing projects languish. Boice (1995) observed that successful writers develop self-discipline and patience.

> Tip 4.4: The best way to lose time is to waste it. Time is a great equalizer—nobody has too much of it. Successful writers do not *have* the time to write, they *make* the time to write Learn to use time as a tool, not an excuse.

Pushing Past the Block

Henson (1990) recommended writing fast to get it down, then adding, subtracting, and modifying later (See Tip 4.5). Many authors set specific, realistic goals for each writing session (Hamilton, 1996). Clark (1994) suggested ending writing with an idea for what to do next. This reduces the anxiety of facing the blank page. Instead, the writer returns with motivation to start again.

Westermann (1994) advised creating an outline for the draft. The outline helps to structure the task so that when the writer bogs down on one section, there are other sections to address. An outline also promotes an integrated whole in which there is a relationship between all sections of the writing. To this effect, the introduction should direct the manuscript toward a unifying theme that finds completion in the conclusion.

Cultivating Creativity

Writers have days when they do not feel particularly insightful, or they feel hopelessly uncreative (See Tip 4.6). Sternberg's (1997) research on intelligence led him to conclude that there are three types of intelligence that can be enhanced: creative, analytical, and practical. He offered hope for cultivating creative intelligence by suggesting people (a) believe in themselves; (b) find what they love to do; (c) capitalize on their strengths; (d)

> Tip 4.5: Pen, pencil, word processor, table, time, and inclination aside, few writers are always eager to write. When a block occurs it sometimes helps to write thoughts rather than convictions; phrases, rather than sentences; and it always helps to write them down fast, then add, subtract, and modify them later.

learn the knowledge base but do not let it confine them; (e) tolerate ambiguity; (f) be willing to take sensible risks; (g) make mistakes and learn from them; (h) allow time to be creative; (i) maintain their sense of humor; (j) persevere in overcoming obstacles; (k) think long term and consider things in a larger context; and (l) ask for other ways to define and solve problems. Garrison Keillor echoes many of these ideas adding, "be bold and thrust forward and have the courage to fail" (in Clark,1994, p. 8).

> Tip 4.6: A blank sheet of paper or a "new" word processing file can be an intimidating start to a creative writing project. Be bold, thrust forward, and have the courage to learn something from failure and write on.

Dispelling Myths of the Evil Editor

Many new writers have conjured an erroneous image of the rejecting editor who feels joy in ripping apart one's best work (See Tip 4.7). Henson's (1990) survey of refereed journals in education revealed that most editors welcome queries from potential authors. As a matter of fact, editors recommend authors write a letter asking if the topic would be of interest to the journal and readership. This letter should demonstrate knowledge of the journal with comments about the type of articles the inquiring author has read that indicate the readership might be interested. Based on personal experience as an editor, Natriello (1996) advised writing to editors but cautioned authors to be courteous even in the face of disappointment. Editors have their own frustrations with the review process. Their reviewers return manuscripts late, and editors often have to respond to complaints about critical feedback and rejection.

Most editors know the difficulty of writing and remember their personal reactions to rejection. These editors are often good teachers and wise counselors (Henson, 1987). They have sound advice concerning how to organize and clarify writing so that it flows. Editors can suggest how to modify a manuscript to conform to their journal. Most beginners write too much. Editors can help to eliminate extra verbiage so that articles are succinct and powerful. Many writers lament not having heeded editors' advice (Clark, 1994). Excessive self-criticism is debilitating but insufficient self-criticism is the handmaiden of mediocrity.

Enlisting Support

Writing can be a lonely endeavor. Some writers prefer to work with others. "When it's good, it's very good"; co-authors may have complementary strengths and may be a source of emotional support. "But, when it's bad, it's awful"; many co-authors find they have incompatible concerns with timelines and commitment to specific tasks. Henson's (1987) advice for co-authors

> *Tip 4.7: Some people believe editors separate the wheat from the chaff and then publish the chaff.* Most editors know the difficulty of writing and remember their personal reactions to rejection. Let them do their thing and be open to learning something from anything they do.

is to develop specific timelines and clarify responsibilities continuously. Co-authors can alternate taking the lead on projects to balance workloads.

Paul, Marfo, and Anderson (1996) described a powerful group structure called Collaborative Research Groups (CRG), which are teams of faculty and doctoral students with shared interests in an area of applied research. The CRG process encourages comparisons of personal experiences and fosters reflection on long-held assumptions. In this instance, group members offer collegial support for completing research tasks and writing through a "writer's guild" established at the University of Wisconsin-Milwaukee. As a result, they implement training for group members in constructive review techniques and develop supportive group responses to common writing roadblocks (Padgett & Begun, 1996).

Even if an author does not write with others, good writers seek the advice of others (See Tip 4.8). Hamilton (1996) recommended finding a mentor who has been successful in publishing. Many senior faculty are honored by the acknowledgment of their talent and the request for their guidance. Boice (1993) indicated that nothing ensures a strong start in successful publication more than mentors and support networks. At the very least, successful writers ask others to read their work, and they accept suggestions as necessary refinement in the development of better manuscripts (Fine, 1988).

New writers must be forthright in asking for help from deans and department chairs. Beginning faculty members should clarify the university expectation for research and publication to develop their personal goals. When setting goals for writing, new faculty members should consider the full range of their responsibilities while at the same time creating a vision for their future careers (which may involve life at another university with different expectations). Based on this information, new faculty members might discuss long-term plans and how the resources of the university could be used to support them. This initiative makes a clear statement of new faculty members' awareness and commitment as well as faculty members' justifiable belief that there should be support throughout the process. This initiative may spur administrators to channel available resources that might have been used for other purposes.

> *Tip 4.8: Sometimes advice is what we ask for when we already know an answer but wish we didn't.* Sometimes we seek approval from others for a course already charted. Most of us don't think much of advice, but even good writers seek the advice of others. The trick is to use advice to generate light more than heat.

Editing Ruthlessly

For many writers, first drafts are often mediocre at best (Westermann, 1994). Clark (1994) cautioned that if you fall in love with a first draft, you greatly enhance the possibilities of never getting it published. Garrison Keillor (in Clark, 1994) wrote, "When in doubt, read it out loud....it helps you know what is bad so you can eliminate it or else use a pseudonym" (p. 3). Westermann (1994) imagined his audience when reading aloud and made notes about what they would not like or what needs to be clarified.

Successful writers ask colleagues with good editing skills to inspect manuscripts for errors. Sometimes an editor's decision to reject rather than revise is based on the presence of multiple errors giving the impression of carelessness. In addition, editors look for manuscripts with good overall organization that ease the work of the reader. Good writers organize content into clear paragraphs and use subheadings (See Tip 4.9).

> *Tip 4.9: Editing may seem like fighting with your own words, but good writers know that writing demands repair.* Be careful not to be too hard and lose the benefit. Remember it is harder to write a short letter than a long one, and the work is in editing.

Submitting Effectively

Writers seeking to publish must get to know the kind of work a journal publishes (See Tip 4.10). And, authors should attempt to match the style of writing to the journal. There are several ways to identify the style of the journal. When reading what has been published, one can examine articles to determine their length, organization, and special features, such as case studies or recommendations for practice. In addition, editors write commentary and statements of interest periodically in the front of the journal.

In terms of the importance of research, readers can assess whether specific journals (a) merely demonstrate an awareness of research in the field, (b) explain the application of research to practice, or (c) actually describe a specific research project. It may be tempting for new authors to brazenly challenge the status quo. This approach risks rejection. Writers may be more successful if they acknowledge tradition and then pose thoughtful questions based on new data.

All journals have published directions for submissions, including format, number of copies, and additional requirements. It surprises editors how many manuscripts are submitted that appear as if the contributing authors have ignored guidelines. Successful writers study directions for submission and follow them explicitly. If a manuscript is returned for revision, successful authors revise. In a conversation among editors (Natriello, 1996), it was revealed that only half of manuscripts returned for revision were resubmitted. Revised manuscripts have a greater chance of publication than first-time submissions. It is important to read editorial suggestions several times to understand fully what the editor and reviewers are seeking. Letters from editors generally indicate which suggestions are critical and which are optional. When returning revised manuscripts, successful writers include letters detailing how concerns were addressed in the revisions. If the writer disagrees with an editorial question or comment, then the rationale should be included as well. This letter, with explanation and rationale, communicates to the editor that the suggestions were valued and carefully considered.

> *Tip 4.10: Understand that every journal is different.* A simple way to ensure failure is to submit a manuscript without considering the purpose, audience, history, content, and style of the journal being considered as the publication source. Successful authors in every area of writing know the kind of work selected sources publish, and they try to cater in every way possible to the direction this information provides to their own work.

A Personal Journey

As a new faculty member, I knew I had to publish. When my department chair asked what topic or research I might write about, I felt like I was looking my worst fear right in the face. I was teaching four new classes and settling my family into a new habitat; plus, it seemed someone always needed me "desperately" whenever I was not in my office. Yet, if I was going to succeed at publishing and at advancing my career, I realized I had to schedule at least two writing mornings a week at home.

I had an idea that intrigued me. As a doctoral student, I had participated in research in which pupils were asked what they remembered at the end of a lesson (Morine-Dershimer, 1991). A colleague and I implemented the research in a middle school comparing responses of students with learning disabilities to responses of their nondisabled peers. A description of the research was submitted to *TEACHING Exceptional Children*. Several months later, we received the feedback that we had a great idea, but the manuscript needed to be completely revised to appeal to the audience of the journal. We revised the article, and it was accepted.

Applying a similar research idea to college students, another manuscript was generated for a research journal in psychology. Months later, the feedback arrived with a three-page rejection letter questioning our method and commenting on our writing. I threw the letter on my department chair's desk and demanded some kind of encouragement. He shared a brief history of his own rejections and acceptances. But, I was inconsolable and refused to reread the letter for a month.

After cooling off, my colleague and I read the letter carefully and saw the wisdom in the comments. We responded to the editorial concerns and resubmitted the manuscript. This time the rejection letter was more encouraging with only two pages of questions and comments. Another revision and a resubmission resulted in a third, short rejection letter complimenting us on our good idea and perseverance but stating that further revision would probably not help the article conform to the journal. We revised the manuscript based on some final comments of that editor and submitted the article to another journal. The editor of this journal responded enthusiastically, accepting the manuscript with minor revisions, and praising its unique conceptualization, well-written style, and appropriateness for their journal.

I took every rejection personally, but I had a passion for sharing my ideas, and I was determined to learn how to write better. Years later, as associate editor of two journals and reviewer for several others, I have come to know editors personally and find them to be hard-working, caring professionals. I also realize the importance of the support offered me at the beginning of my career. There were a few colleagues who were always willing to listen, provide encouragement, and critique ideas. In addition, my most notable publications were co-authored. Although co-authoring was rarely simple, the synergism always resulted in superior manuscripts.

Writing for publication tests self-confidence every step of the way, yet I know of no more effective process to clarify my thoughts and share my ideas with other educators. Finally, writing continues to be a fascinating, ever-unfolding journey.

References

Boice, R. (1992). *The new faculty member.* San Francisco: Jossey-Bass.

Boice, R. (1993). Early turning points in professional careers of women and minorities. *New Directions for Teaching and Learning, 53,* 71-79.

Clark, T. (1994). 100 tips from bestselling writers. *Writer's Digest, 74*(8), 24-30.

Fine, G. A. (1988). The ten commandments of writing. *American Sociologist, 19,* 152-157.

Hamilton, K. S. (1996). *Acceptance of new and junior faculty into four-year institutions of higher education: An annotated bibliography.* Annotated bibliography. (ERIC Document Reproduction Service No. ED 396 619)

Henson, K. T. (1987). Writing for professional publication. *Phi Delta Kappa Fastback #262.* (ERIC Document Reproduction Service No. ED 292 110)

Henson, K. T. (1990). Writing for education journals. *Phi Delta Kappa, 71,* 800-803.

Morine-Dershimer, G. (1991). Learning to think like a teacher. *Teaching & Teacher Education, 7,* 159-168.

Natriello, G. (1996). Lessons for young scholars seeking to publish. *Teachers College Record, 97,* 509-517.

Padgett, D. L., & Begun, A. L. (1996). The writer's guild: A model of support for social work faculty. *Journal of Social Work Education, 32,* 237-244.

Paul, J. L., Duchnowski, A. J., & Danforth, S. (1993). Changing the way we do our business: One department's story of collaboration with public schools. *Teacher Education and Special Education, 16,* 95-109.

Paul, J. L., Marfo, K., & Anderson, J. A. (1996) . Developing an ethos for change in a department of special education: Focus on collaboration and an ethic of care. *Teacher Education and Special Education, 19*(2), 133-146.

Rechtien, J. G., (1997). A note on measuring apprehension about writing. *Psychological Reports, 80,* 907-913.

Renegar, S. L. (1993). *Writing for publication: Are junior faculty prepared?* General Informational analysis. (ERIC Document Reproduction Service No. ED 369 374)

Sternberg, R. (1997, October). *Cultivating creativity.* Keynote speech at the annual conference of the Council for Learning Disabilities, Arlington, VA.

Westermann, J. (1994). Lessons I've learned. *Writer's Digest, 74,* 300-303.

Chapter 5

Being Successful in the Academy

Robert Rueda, Shariba Rivers Kyles, and Kofi Lomotey

What is there that confers the noblest delight? What is that which swells a man's breast with pride above that which any other experience can bring to him? Discovery! To know that you are walking where none others have walked; that you are beholding what human eye has not seen before; that you are breathing a virgin atmosphere. To give birth to an idea, to discover a great thought, an intellectual nugget, right under the dust of a field that many a brain-plough had gone over before. To find a new planet, to invent a new hinge, to find a way to make the lightning carry your messages. To be the first—that is the idea.

—*Mark Twain*

Gender bias notwithstanding, Twain's comment is important. Research means answering questions that have not been answered. Those who conduct research know the intoxication of discovery and, with it, they know the dissemination expectations of the academy in which they participate in professional development activities. Educational researchers have a primary responsibility to distribute scientific information and other scholarly products, not unlike researchers in the physical and natural sciences. One of the more difficult challenges for scholars in higher education—students and their instructors alike—is mastery of the communicative conventions that characterize written discourse, that is, writing used in theses, dissertations, and later manuscripts submitted for publication in academic journals. Many students in advanced degree programs have significant difficulty in integrating these conventions into the scholarly products that they are required to produce as part of their educational training and professional development. Often novice students in advanced degree programs assume that writing proficiency in nonacademic domains which they may have previously mastered is easily generalized and that little or no new attention or effort needs to be paid to mastering writing apart from those abilities that they already possess (Obiakor, Lomotey, & Rueda, 1997).

Academic/scholarly writing is a unique type of discourse. Because of this, not only do students encounter difficulties, but upon entering the profession they find it difficult to convert their scholarly pieces into manuscripts. In many ways, writing according to the conventions within the academy is like learning a second language. Like any discourse system, it has its own form and function. While most students are proficient in the conversational nuances and informality of everyday oral language, academic writing requires logical, systematic, precise, focused, direct, and abstract skills that often are not well-practiced. The different forms and functions of academic writing are briefly discussed below followed by sections directing key aspects of the academic writing process. This content is intended to assist with writing within the limitations of the dissertation research and converting it to help fulfill publishing requirements within the academy.

Form of Academic Discourse

Like any discourse system, academic writing is rule-governed with its own internally consistent and widely agreed-on conventions. In the discipline of social sciences, the primary source for these conventions is found in the *Publication Manual of the American Psychological Association* (American Psychological Association, 1994). The basic mechanics for academic writing are comprehensively covered in this document, and most publications in the discipline of education require and follow these conventions. Although the details of these conventions are beyond the scope of this chapter, those who plan to make a career in an academic setting or who will be engaging in scholarly writing should become familiar with this publication as early on as is practical.

Although the basic mechanics of scholarly writing are important, it is not this dimension which scholars tend to find most problematic. The basic issue is that scientific writing differs from literary or informal writing. Specifically, clear communication, rather than effect, should be the overarching characteristic of writing for an academic audience (See Tip 5.1). The APA Manual (1994), for instance, places particular importance on the orderly presentation of ideas, smoothness of expression, economy of expression, and precision and clarity, versus clutter. As Zinsser (1990), succinctly put it, writers must:

- "Aim for continuity in words, concepts, and thematic development from the opening statement to the conclusion" (p. 24);
- "Aim for clear logical communication" (p. 25);
- "Say only what needs to be said" (p. 26);
- "Make certain every word means exactly what you intend it to mean" (p. 28).

Tip 5.1: Communicate logically and clearly. Orderly and precise communication is an important characteristic of good writing.

Function of Academic Discourse

Although dissemination is a primary purpose of academic writing, and presentation of research findings is one of the more common functions served by it, there are other reasons to write as well. In addition to empirical research reports, for example, academic writing might include theoretical analyses, reviews of literature, and other formats which might not focus strictly on the presentation of empirical data but instead on reaching a broader/different audience. This would require the scholar to convert research into terms that others outside of the scholar's area of expertise would understand. Indeed, some argue that all academic writing should be understandable by lay people (Obiakor et al., 1997). Although specific issues of format might differ slightly in these types of publications, the general principles of style related to academic writing, such as clarity of expression and precision, are still critical and ensure that the quality of the research and manuscript is not compromised.

Traditionally, the primary audience for scholarly dissemination has been, not surprisingly, other scholars. Tenure and academic careers, after all, often hinge on the evaluation of one's scholarly products by peers in the field. Many scholars often tend to avoid nonacademic sources because they are deemed to be of lesser value and importance than academic outlets. "Popular" publication outlets, for example, do not often have the same stringent quality controls such as those found in first-rate refereed journals. Sometimes they exist for different purposes, such as to promote a particular point of view, to create controversy, or even to maximize commercial sales. However, pressure is increasingly being placed on researchers and scholars to widen the targets of their dissemination efforts. More and more, scholars are preparing manuscripts for more than one audience (See Tip 5.2). Academics are being made increasingly aware of the importance of the public (broadly conceived) as a critical audience. For example, research funding is often tied to public perceptions of the value of research to recognizable and important problems. Increased pressure is being placed on researchers to think about their work in light of important social problems and public policy issues (Obiakor & Algozzine, 1995). This tension is likely to increase rather than decrease, and is an issue that those entering the field, and those who have just recently entered the field, have to face early in their careers.

> Tip 5.2: *Write for more than one audience even when your topic is specific.* Try many publication outlets. In other words, do not put all your eggs in one basket. Spread the word to extend the message.

Dissertations and Published Articles

The luxury of writing strictly for academic peers is disappearing quickly although the responsibility to address issues from a scholarly perspective is not—this widely held perception is slowly disappearing. Put simply, it is that scholarly or intelligent writing is evaluated based upon the length of the words and sentences. In reality, the worth of writing is measured by the degree to which the reader can understand that which you have written. Dissertations and articles are two forms of academic writing that require similar but different writing approaches. Submitting an article based on the dissertation is often the first writing experience for many professionals after graduate school. To facilitate such an effort, it is helpful to recognize a few similarities and differences between dissertations and published articles. Key differences revolve around purpose and conventions of writing.

Dissertations are written primarily to demonstrate competence in research skills to a committee of peers and to contribute to knowledge as a result of the process. The format and writing style are structured, focused, and highly academic (i.e., directed by tradition and graduate school guidelines). Most professionals prepare one dissertation and seldom use it as a model for subsequent writing. Articles are written primarily to extend what is known in an academic discipline. The strict conventions required in dissertations (e.g., chapters with sometimes redundant content) are not required in articles and expectations regarding selectivity of content, economy of expression, and restraint of discussion are particularly germane (cf. APA, 1994). Similarities between dissertations and articles are evident in concepts that drive the selection of a research topic.

Selecting a Research Topic

Two questions most often asked in the context of students beginning to think about dissertations and research projects are: How does one generate a research topic that will eventually lead to publishable products? and What are some criteria that should guide the selection of a suitable topic? The following are guidelines that have proven useful at this stage of the research process.

First, the topic should be important. Importance is defined in terms of the literature and theory in which it is grounded. That is, important research extends the current knowledge base and tells the academic world something that is not already known. This is why a thorough and critical review of the existing literature is a necessary first step in the process. Pointing out gaps in existing research, methodological errors, or shortcomings provides a strong foundation for demonstrating how a research project (i.e., dissertation or other study) will fit in and add to the existing related literature. In addition, ideally, research should address a theoretical or practical problem. This is especially critical given the increasing demand to show the relevance of one's research to current educational issues.

There are areas in research that can be unpopular. These areas include, but are not limited to, topics that do not fall within the mainstream curricula of the disciplines; topics that primarily deal with African-Americans, Asian-Americans, Native Americans and women; and exclusive, noncomparative studies of any of the aforementioned groups. Although, on the surface, this may be discouraging news to some, we believe there are legitimate justifications for doing "unpopular" research. One reason is that ethnic/racial and gender groups are distinctive and present significant researchable challenges in society. These groups are worthy of study simply because of this fact. Another justification for doing "unpopular" research is that the absence of a comparison group is not necessarily a limitation. Rather, particularly in qualitative research, focused study on a group can provide more intimate details of behaviors or customs, without imposing definitions from outside groups onto the studied group.

Throughout history, anthropologists, for example, have purposely studied distinct groups (Obiakor et al., 1997).

Another criterion frequently considered when selecting a research topic for a dissertation or other study is whether or not the topic falls within reasonable limits with regard to practicality, time, and resources. Many students attempt to design their first study to address myriad complex questions and to address numerous social, policy, and theoretical issues simultaneously. Often the scope of the work would require tremendous financial resources, extensive personnel, and several years of sustained effort. Doing such work is not feasible for most students or other professionals engaged in other full-time experiences. Generally, the best advice is to defer the fame and riches that are assumed to be associated with such a monumental contribution in favor of conducting a reasonable project that can be completed in light of typical expectations and limitations. This is not to argue for diminished quality or importance with respect to a topic, but more to reflect that research needs to be realistic.

Developing scholars should keep in mind that the selected topic should be in an area in which they have a general interest and in which they would like to be considered experts (See Tip 5.3). Normally, projects such as dissertations and writing for publication require a major intellectual (as well as time) investment. The burden is often eased when the area represents a personal and professional interest. Moreover, if the topic is one that has many facets, interest is heightened and converting a dissertation or single project report into a manuscript (or several manuscripts) for publication is facilitated.

An important source for finding research topics and problems on which to write is the literature in one's area of interest. Generally, topics arise from critical and reflective reading in a given area. Critical analysis often leads one to identify gaps in the literature and other shortcomings that would argue for a study to be carried out. If students begin to learn to read critically early on in their coursework, by the time they are ready to engage in independent research, they will have an abundance of important questions to pursue.

Role of critical analysis. The use of reflective reading to identify where research is lacking in certain areas is only one purpose of critical analysis. A characteristic that distinguishes academic publications from other types of outlets is quality control. How is this achieved in academic publications? The primary strategy is to rely on peer review of scholarly products. Every journal that uses peer review lists the editor and editorial advisory board, normally made up of recognized scholars in the area. When manuscripts are received, they are sent by the editor to peer reviewers who evaluate the content from an academic perspective. This includes factors such as the appropriateness of the theoretical basis of a study, the relevance of the literature in which the study is grounded, the suitability of the manuscript for the particular publication, and the appropriateness of the methods and analysis (cf. APA, 1994). Typically, with high quality scholarly journals, the process is "blind" (i.e., the identity of the author is not known to the reviewers and vice versa). Following the reviews, the editor then typically makes a decision on whether to publish the manuscript, asks for revisions based on the reviews, suggests a more appropriate outlet, or simply rejects the contribution. Although the review criteria for manuscripts that are not empirical research reports may differ slightly, the element of peer review is still critical. With other publications, there may be no peer review, and the editor will make an independent decision.

The process of critical peer review should not be seen as adversarial. It is—theoretically—a mechanism to obtain an unbiased analysis of one's ideas and work. Many novice writers have difficulty with this aspect of scholarly writing and the process is seen as threatening. This often results in diminished motivation to write or else prevents writing altogether. What is critical to realize is that, in most instances, it is the ideas that are being held up to critical scrutiny not one's personality, intelligence, or worth as a person. It is important not to take criticism negatively, since it is not directed at you as a person. It is a tool that expert writers use to sharpen their ideas, present their arguments in a clearer or more understandable way, or even to gain new insights and develop new and interesting questions. It is critical to realize that the dialectical process is what advances understanding, and therefore it should be welcomed, not shunned (Obiakor et al., 1997).

Having discussed issues of form and function related to academic writing and some similarities and differences in written products prepared for the academy, final areas of consideration for novice writers are how to improve one's writing ability and how to foster writing ability in others. Each is discussed in the following sections.

> Tip 5.3: *Select a research topic dear to you.* Energy and interest communicated in a manuscript carry weight in the review process. Value reviews but don't take them too personally.

Becoming a Better Writer

Learning to write in the academy can be compared, in many ways, to the process that young non-English speaking students go through in acquiring English skills. Academic writing can be seen as a second language, a special type of literacy which may build on existing proficiency but which differs in important ways as well. It is as much a process of socialization into a "community of practice" as learning new skills (Pease-Alvarez & Vasquez, 1994). What, then, is the mechanism through which it occurs?

One answer emanates from the work of theorists who deal with young children's language and literacy. Krashen (1989), for example, emphasized the role of comprehensible input in low-anxiety contexts as a primary element in promoting language and literacy acquisition. Comprehensible input, in this case, means engaging with text that is understandable and meaningful. In academic writing, this notion can be translated to mean that novice writers should spend a great deal of time reading academic materials of the type they would like to produce (i.e., always searching for models to guide subsequent work). When one develops an area of research interest, reading academic materials in that area takes on a more personal, authentic, and meaningful character. With increasing knowledge and expertise in that specific area of interest, including familiarity with specialized vocabulary, key theoreticians and researchers, and "hot topics," reading should become not only more comprehensible but more meaningful as well. This should form an important bridge into proficiency as an academic writer.

Other language theorists have extended Krashen's (1989) framemwork to include comprehensible output as well (Cummins, 1994; Swain, 1986). In the present context, this can be taken to mean that in order to move from being a novice writer to being an expert writer, one needs to practice writing that involves two parts: writing and re-writing. The easiest way to accomplish this goal is to get involved in projects and activities that will lead to products that can be disseminated to academic audiences. These projects should be given to several people for review before the final copy is issued. Peer review is an important step in the writing process as it affords the writer the opportunity to "try out" the piece on a sample audience before final production. Whether or not the audience can comprehend and logically follow the author's ideas is an important aspect of good writing skills and leads to scholarly excellence. Ideally, these projects and activities would build on the area of interest that the student is beginning to develop and would subsequently lead to theses, dissertations, and other dissemination products.

A final factor to consider is the beliefs one holds about writing, oneself as a writer, and the role that writing plays in important life activities (See Tip 5.4). These are often formed when one becomes a member of the community of academic writers. Researchers are increasingly aware that personal beliefs are an important mediator of behavior. Beliefs about the role of writing are especially critical. Drawing on the language-learning metaphor again, it is instructive to examine the role of oral language in children's everyday activities. In acquiring a first language, children do not consciously "learn language" for its own sake; rather it is a tool embedded in activities they want to accomplish. In a similar fashion, it is important to realize that academic writing is a tool, that is, a means to an end and not an end in itself. Academic writing should not be viewed as something to be mastered for a purpose external to meaningful activities. It should be seen as a tool to inform, ignite interest, stimulate conversation, and assist in problem-solving. It is a step on the road to continuous professional development in becoming a scholar.

Tip 5.4: *You must hold positive beliefs about writing, yourself as a writer, and the role that writing plays in important life activities.* Writing is hard work. Be as positive as you can throughout the writing process.

Assisting Others in Academic Writing

Recent advances in sociocultural theory provide a useful framework on which to draw for thinking about the process of becoming literate in "academese." Although an extensive treatment of this framework is beyond the scope of this chapter, a brief description of some key elements can help demonstrate the usefulness of this approach.

Sociocultural theory focuses on the social and cultural aspects of learning and cognitive development. Learning is seen as a process in which the learner interacts with a "more com-

petent other," in the learner's "zone of proximal development." This is simply the difference between what the learner can achieve independently in contrast to what can be achieved with appropriate assistance (See Tip 5.5). In this model, teaching is redefined as providing "assisted performance" to a learner within the learner's "zone." This model has often been described as an apprenticeship model, similar in many ways to the enculturation process that takes place when a junior craftsperson is being socialized into a trade or profession. The general goal of this joint activity is to assist the learner to move from the initial stages of "other-regulation" to self-regulation. Just like a young child engaging in storybook reading with a parent, the novice takes over more and more of the responsibility for the task until eventually she or he can accomplish it independently (Forman, Minick, & Stone, 1993; Tharp & Gallimore, 1988).

Operating from a model of assisted performance, Tharp (1993) outlined seven basic means of assisting performance. These include:

1. Modeling—offering behavior for imitation. This might be in the form of reading academic materials or modeling the writing process one engages in during the process of creating a manuscript for publication.

2. Feedback —providing information on a performance as it compares to a standard. This can be informal feedback by colleagues or more formal feedback such as that provided by a journal editor.

3. Contingency management—using principles of reinforcement and punishment. Often the professional recognition that one receives for important ideas or scholarly products is highly reinforcing, especially in the early stages of one's academic career. The punishment for failing to produce scholarly works often means denial of promotion and/or tenure in the academic setting.

4. Instruction—ascertaining which specific actions are necessary to complete a task. Sometimes direct instruction *in the context of producing a meaningful product* is the best means of assisting one's writing. Instruction can refer to the organization of ideas, format (especially when writing for a specific publisher), or other aspects such as suitability of topic for specific audiences.

5. Questioning—requesting a response for impartial readers/reviewers. Sometimes, the questions one receives in the course of formal or informal feedback are excellent means of improving one's written products.

6. Cognitive structuring—providing explanations to questions raised by outside readers. This can help the writer organize and justify new learning and belief structures. It also makes the writer actively think about what has been written and how it can be improved.

7. Task structuring—chunking, segregating, sequencing or otherwise structuring a task into or from components. After the pertinent questions have been answered and the author has mentally reviewed the project, this is the final step in the writing project. The organization of the document may need altering in order to present a smooth, coherent final product.

In the context of coaching one to become an experienced or expert writer, the best means of providing the types of assistance outlined above is within the context of joint productive activity—namely, a piece of academic writing. The type and amount of assisted performance provided will necessarily depend upon close monitoring of the zone of proximal development of the individual writer. In general, however, these means of assisting performance provide a useful specification of tools which can move a novice to an expert writer.

> *Tip 5.5: Enjoy joint productive writing activity.* Assist people and ask for assistance when necessary. Share the pluses and minuses to make the whole experience more productive.

Continuing a Work in Progress

After finishing the dissertation, the scholar may find it to his or her advantage to begin looking at publishing opportunities. The best place to start would be with the dissertation itself. However, the task is not easy; yet it is not as hard as one would think. Essentially, what is being asked of the new professional is to take a book full of facts, figures, and explanations of statistical methodologies and turn it into a reader-friendly manuscript that a broader audience will understand. Although this sounds daunting in the beginning, one must consider the more positive aspects of this task: (a) the topic has already been selected, (b) it has been thoroughly researched, (c) it is a topic with which the author is extremely familiar, and, (d) it is almost already written! The three main steps to getting an article published involve conceptualizing, preparing drafts, and finding a suitable source. If the scholar is starting with the dissertation, the conceptualizing and some of the writing are already done.

What needs to be accomplished in transforming a dissertation into an article is putting what is already written into a more appropriate form. More often than not, the dissertation has a very narrow focus, is usually written in an impersonal and unbiased tone, has a language that is common only among the professionals within the field, and has an extensive section dedicated solely to the review of previous literature related to the subject. The following suggestions address how to modify the dissertation in a form for future publication.

1. *Amplify the context of your research.* The layperson usually wants to deal not so much with how the research was conducted, but why. It would also help to personalize the research by using language that more easily tells a story instead of states the facts. Using this method allows for more personal observation and helps the reader relate more readily to the topic.

2. *Modify the literature review.* Simply put, if it is not directly associated with what you are trying to say delete it. An extensive literature review, to anyone, but especially laypeople, is exhausting and boring. The style of a manuscript must flow to keep the reader interested. Weighing the reader down with what researchers said or did many years ago will quickly act as a stimulus for the reader to quit reading. The author must strive to present importance, need, and relevance with enough breadth and clarity so the study will be understood by a wide professional audience. The author must also consider optimizing the focus of the method section. Although extremely important in the academic writing, the details of how the au-

thor conducted the research (e.g., who was contacted, the details of letters requesting permission, and human subjects, committee forms) are usually not considered appropriate or essential in a journal article. If there is a question about relevance or need, authors often suggest they be contacted for additional details.

3. *Minimize tables, footnotes, and quotations.* In order to achieve a smooth, flowing writing style, the author should try to keep tables and footnotes to a minimum. Placing tables and footnotes in the center of the manuscript, on the page following its reference, or at the bottom of the page distracts the reader and interrupts the reading process. Place the tables in the back if you find that they are absolutely necessary. Instead of footnotes, try endnotes. Quotations should be minimized as they, too, can distract the reader.

After changes have been made, it is always a good idea to have other people, within the author's field and outside of his or her field, read the text. These "reviewers" should provide critical feedback that should include, at a minimum, the manuscript's strongest and weakest points, suggestions for improving the overall readability of the text, errors in punctuation or grammar, and comments about the organization of the manuscript. This feedback will prove beneficial to the author in making necessary changes and with ensuring that the quality of the work is not understated.

The public audience is a growing entity with regard to academic writing. It might serve the author/researcher well in terms of further research funding to tailor the manuscript so that both the public and academic audiences can appreciate it. Learning to write while "straddling the fence" will be difficult at first. However, with the aid of those colleagues who are already published—the developing author/researcher will be able to learn and make the transition more easily. The key is to identify scholars who have been successful in effectively communicating to varying audiences and to model one's work in a similar fashion.

Perspective on Writing in the Academy

We believe writers are made, not born. There are many strategies one can use to develop as a writer. Even though one may be proficient in some areas of writing, there are special conventions and purposes for academic writing which often require special attention. When one realizes that writing is an important tool that facilitates participation in the academic community, sees peer review as a way to enhance the clarity and power of one's ideas, and actively pursues important and personally meaningful questions and issues, the challenge of mastering academic writing should be much more surmountable. In essence, we believe good writing is a critical element of good scholarship and professional development; we also believe there are more reasons to write than reasons not to write.

Most publishers accept authors' word choices unless they are obviously inaccurate. What you write conveys a message and can provide an effective means of instructing beyond the content you are discussing in your work. If your writing reflects respect for individuals you are writing about and your readers, you will contribute to continued use of unbiased language in human interactions. You must strive for appropriate levels of accuracy and specificity. For example, using *man* to refer to all human beings is not as accurate as using *men and women*. Similarly, "some people interpret gay as referring to men and women, whereas others interpret the term as including only men (for clarity, *gay men* and *lesbians* currently are preferred)" (APA, 1994, p. 47). When discussing disabilities, put people first (e.g., child with a disability, not disabled child; individuals with mental retardation, not mentally retarded individuals), avoid labeling people by their disability or exaggerating its severity (e.g., children with learning disabilities rather than the learning disabled, individuals with epilepsy rather than epileptics), and use emotionally neutral phrases (e.g., uses a wheelchair, not confined to a wheelchair) to communicate positive aspects of individual differences (APA, 1994; Boston, 1992; CEC, 1997).

To be sure, writing for the academy is unlike other forms of expression. With practice and a little help from our friends, it can be a positive, rewarding experience. The goal is simple: Share discovery with clear, precise communication; the outcome unbound.

References

American Psychological Association. (1994). *Publication manual of the American Psychological Association.* (4th Ed.). Washington, DC: Author.

Boston, B. O. (1992, November). Portraying people with disabilities: Toward a new vocabulary. *The Editorial Eye, 15,* 1-3, 6-7.

The Council for Exceptional Children. (1997). *Policy statement on people first language.* Reston, VA: Author.

Cummins, J. (1994). Knowledge, power, and identity in teaching English as a second language. In F. Genesee (Ed.), *Educating second language children: The whole child, the whole curriculum, the whole community* (pp. 33-58). New York: Cambridge University Press.

Forman, E. A., Minick, N., & Stone, C. A. (1993). *Contexts for learning: Sociocultural dynamics in children's development.* New York: Oxford University Press.

Krashen, S. (1989). *Language acquisition and language education.* New York: Prentice-Hall International.

Obiakor, F. E., & Algozzine, B. (1995). *Managing problem behaviors: Perspectives for general and special educators.* Dubuque, IA: Kendall/Hunt.

Obiakor, F. E., Lomotey, K., & Rueda, R. (1997, January). *Writing for publication.* Paper presented at the Multicultural Symposium of the Division for Culturally and Linguistically Diverse Exceptional Learners (DDEL), The Council for Exceptional Children, New Orleans, LA.

Pease-Alvarez, C., & Vasquez, O. (1994). Language socialization in ethnic minority communities. In F. Genesee (Ed.), *Educating second language children: The whole child, the whole curriculum, the whole community* (pp.82-102). New York: Cambridge University Press.

Swain, M. (1986). Communicative competence: Some roles of comprehensible input and comprehensible output in its development. In J. Cummins & M. Swain (Eds.), *Bilingualism in education: Aspects of theory, research and practice.* London: Longman.

Tharp, R. (1993). Institutional and social context of educational practice and reform. In E. A. Forman, N. Minick, & C. A. Stone (Eds.), *Contexts for learning: Sociocultural dynamics in children's development* (pp. 269-282). New York: Oxford University.

Tharp, R. G., & Gallimore, R. (1988). *Rousing minds to life: Teaching, learning, and schooling in a social context.* New York: Cambridge University Press.

Zinsser, W. (1990). *On writing well: An informal guide to writing nonfiction.* New York: Harper Perennial.

Chapter 6

Writing Books, Materials, and Other Professional Products

Jean N. Boston and James R. Patton

During creation there was placed within your soul a vision. It is your only mission this lifetime to go within and retrieve it. You are on a glorious quest to realms where your imagination shall reign supreme, but it is through your heart that you will be shown the way.
—Dorien Israel (1987)

A glorious quest. Doesn't that sound exciting? Throughout this book, you have been reminded that once you begin to publish, you will have launched yourself onto a path for which you will become recognized. Be sure you choose the path where your vision lies. There is nothing sadder than to come to the end of a career and realize that all the effort you expended and the reputation you have built is not really in the area of your passion, but simply someone else's path that you got started on because your dissertation or some other project launched you in a certain direction. On the other hand, there is nothing more rewarding than being creative in the area of your passion. You will not mind crafting your work to the highest level of clarity and impeccability when you love the work that you are doing. With this wisdom as a caveat, you are ready for some tips on how to get published and be financially rewarded.

Typical Scenario

You may have published a number of research articles in your area of expertise but feel the desire to translate the information you have been gathering into a product that teachers or parents can use. "Best Practices," when they are presented in everyday language, are among the most sought-after products. But, these types of products may be harder than you think to develop if you have been schooled in the style and language of the researcher. With commitment and determination, however, those barriers can be overcome. The enticing question continues to be: Who is in a better position to tell what works than you?

Let's assume you have been doing research in the area of transition skills and you have isolated five skills that seem to be essential for successful transitioning to adult life. One of those skills has to do with the use of technology for competitive employment. You have done a search for products for teachers in ECER and in various vocational and computer databases. You have searched ERIC for reports from federally funded projects designed to equip students with disabilities with basic computer skills, and you have found almost no resources in this area. You are pretty sure that there is a need for a curriculum that will help students with cognitive disabilities master some basic computer skills that will allow them to perform several routine jobs required by most businesses. You have done a study with a group of students with severe learning disabilities and mild mental retardation and are convinced that it is possible for these students to learn what they need to be competitive. You have even out-

lined a curriculum that focuses on the essential skills for data entry. These ideas appear to be very marketable. If so, where do you take them for publication?

You will want to submit your idea or product to publishers who market to the special education teacher, and more specifically, to publishers who are interested and already publish curricular products that deal with life skills and work skills. The remainder of this chapter provides guidelines for accomplishing the task of getting your ideas into print.

Recommendations for Submitting Your Product or Idea

Finding a Potential Publisher

Once you have an idea about the area of the profession where you want to make your mark, you need to find a publisher that includes your niche in their line of products. As part of your early planning process, you must write down a clear statement of what you want to accomplish with your product, and what audience you want to communicate with. Ultimately, it is the audience factor that weighs heavily in most publication decisions. Next, you want to determine and analyze other materials that are comparable to yours. The fact that other materials exist should not deter one in pursuing their publication dream; however, it is important to distinguish what makes your product different.

Many of the publishers in special education are well-known to most professionals. However, if one does not know who the publishers are, a little research might be needed (See Tip 6.1). One excellent source of information on books and other media that can be searched by topics is *Exceptional Child Education Resources (ECER)*. This is a quarterly abstract journal that can be accessed by CD-ROM or online (contact Silver Platter at info@silverplatter.com). It is probable that you have been collecting resources in your area of interest and have already established a personal library of books and articles. The references in these resources can provide the names of companies that publish in your area of interest. A range of different types of publishers exists. In addition to established commercial publishers, small publishing houses as well as associations and college-based publishers are viable outlets for your proposed product. A very important point is that every publisher has specific primary and secondary markets. You need to decide clearly who is the audience for your product and, then, select a publisher who sees this audience as one of their primary markets. A useful suggestion is to get a good feel for the types of products that a publisher has in their product lines by checking out their print or online catalogs.

> Tip 6.1: *Conduct research to know publishers suitable for the kind of work you intend to publish.* Preferences are an important part of commercial publishing decisions. Don't go about the business of writing without important information.

Initial Contact

Publishers are always eager to find new product ideas that will complement an already successful product line. Even though the probability of an unsolicited manuscript eventually being published is low, the chances of this happening are increased by having some initial contact with the publisher (See Tip 6.2). The reason many product ideas are rejected as soon as they arrive at a publisher's office is that they do not match the product lines of a company. We recommend that you select several potential publishers and lay out a sample section from your materials that is modeled along the lines of the products they publish.

With a clear vision in mind of what you would like your product to look like, you should call, e-mail, or query by letter the publisher. Specifically, you want to speak with the person who is in charge of the acquisition of new products (e.g., acquisitions editor). This contact provides you the opportunity to (a) determine very quickly whether your product fits the publisher; (b) sense the initial interest of the publisher in your product; (c) establish a personal contact within the publishing company; and (d) obtain guidelines for submitting a prospectus (i.e., document containing information about your proposed product) and other relevant information about the company (e.g., a style sheet, a company mission statement, strategic plan, or list of topics that are targeted for publication).

If a publisher does not have guidelines for developing a prospectus or a style sheet for use, the author should follow the style set forth in the *Publication Manual of the American Psychological Association* (1994) or develop a prospectus that contains the following dimensions: title of product; overview of material (purpose, rationale, and scope); target audience(s); table of contents including outlines of proposed chapters or sections, if possible, and list of contributors (if an edited work); significant features of the material; comparison to competing materials; estimate length of finished product; and estimated completion date.

> Tip 6.2: *Take advantage of your initial contact with a publisher to sense the publisher's interest, establish personal rapport, and gain knowledge about publishing guidelines.* Clearly, first impressions are important. Use them to your advantage.

Submitting a Prospectus—Show That You Have Done Your Homework

The packet of material that you should submit to a publisher should include a cover letter, the prospectus, samples of the material, and information related to qualifications of the author(s) (See Tip 6.3). You need to be meticulous about your submission and be sure that there are no typos in the material you are sending. Professional editors see those kinds of details like no others, and careless errors will bring into question the impeccability of your entire project. The cover letter provides an opportunity to reintroduce your idea, if you have had previous contact, or introduce your idea for the first time, if there was no earlier correspondence. When sending the material to a person to whom you communicated previously, you should be sure to remind him or her of the earlier contact. The letter should briefly summarize the nature of the product you are submitting for consideration and convey why you have a passion for the subject, without overdoing it. Additionally, you should indicate how you came to select them as a potential publisher for your work, elaborating how your product fits with their existing product line and with their overall mission as you understand it. You should be sure you are knowledgeable of the publisher's mission, if you decide to address this issue. You should also be able to obtain this information either from a published mission statement or from your knowledge of their other products.

The packet you submit to publishers must respond to the following questions:

- What is the general topic area(s) of your proposed product?
- How does the topic fit the publisher's product line?
- What do you want them to learn?
- Why do you think there is a need for the product?
- What products are already available on this topic? How is yours different? What is the source of the content?
- What is your personal experience/expertise in this area?
- How will people use the product (curriculum, reference, training manual)?
- Why would the selected publisher be the best one to produce your product?

> Tip 6.3: *When you submit your proposal packet to the publishing company, respond to critical questions that were asked.* Specific answers help sell your ideas and products.

Major Considerations Affecting a Publisher's Decision to Publish a Book or Material

Four Key Questions

Essentially, there are four key questions that a publisher needs to ask about any product being considered for publication. A favorable decision regarding publication will depend on affirmative answers to each of these questions.

1. Does the proposed product fit one of our primary markets?
2. Does the proposed product have merit (i.e., is it good)?
3. Does the proposed product have marketability?
4. Does the proposed product have any features that interfere with its publication (e.g., high production costs and expensive components)?

What can and does happen is that a publisher will receive a prospectus on a wonderful product (high rating related to question #2) but it does not fit a primary market of the publisher. As a result, the decision to publish the product must be a negative one.

Factors a Publisher Must Consider

A well-written, sound, interesting, and appropriately submitted manuscript is not the only consideration operative in selecting products for publication. The preprint costs of editing, typesetting, designing (i.e., page layout, cover, other graphics), along with the costs of printing 2,000 copies of a 100-page book will cost between $5,000 and $8,000, depending upon the detail involved and the physical quality of the publication. As one can deduce, the production costs increase for books with more pages. These costs are divided by the number of copies printed so the unit cost, in this example, would be between $2.50 and $4.00. The industry standard for markup is a factor of 7.5 to 8 times the combined production and printing cost. This markup covers the review process, marketing, a variety of overhead costs, warehousing, customer service, royalties, staff time, and hopefully some profit. The price for this product would be between $18.75 and $30.00. The publisher has to make a judgment about whether the product will sell at the projected price (See Tip 6.4). A decision also has to be made about how many units can be expected to sell the first 12 to 18 months, the recommended limit for estimating a print run. If we take the above example and believe only 1,000 books will sell in the first 18 months, the unit cost would increase to between $5.00 and $8.00, and the retail price would be between $37.50 and $60.00. Even though some reference books, reports, and textbooks are priced in this range, most publishers would not be able to stay in business if the majority of their titles were that expensive, as most teachers are unwilling to spend that much money on a book. A publisher has to price books competitively with other products of similar size and content within their own product line as well as remaining competitive with the pricing of other publishers.

The pricing for curricular materials and other products such as tests usually is higher. This is due to two major factors: (1) They are often multi-component products that are more costly to produce; and (2) the costs of development are more expensive, which are then passed on to the consumer.

> *Tip 6.4: Publishers do not publish what they cannot sell.* You should know that the decision to publish material is highly dependent on the product's marketability.

Publication Process

Different publishers have different procedures. In general, however, the overall sequence of steps in the publication process is similar across publishers. Large commercial publishers have a staff of editors, each in charge of a different specialty area of product line. Midsize and smaller commercial publishers have a staff as well, although it is smaller and there may only be one editor in charge of acquisitions and product development. Publication programs within professional associations, such as The Council for Exceptional Children, will have a staff person who is in charge of editorial matters. The publication process can be divided into three distinct phases: decision to publish, manuscript development, and production (see Figure 6.1). Each of these stages has its own goals and activities and knowledge of the process associated with each of these stages is useful for potential authors.

Figure 6.1
Overview of the Publication Process

Decision to Publish

Certain substantive aspects of this part of the publication process have already been discussed because of their importance to developing a prospectus. However, the procedural aspects of decision making have not. In general, once a prospectus and any accompanying materials are received, an acknowledgment of receipt of the materials will be sent.

In most publishing houses, the acquisition editor has the authority to accept or reject a product proposal based on obvious content and marketing factors. A review process is invoked for proposals that survive the initial screening. Large and small publishers use a peer review process that involves in-house staff and/or outside reviewers. The purpose of this process is to get a reasonable feel for the quality of the proposed product (i.e., question #2 above). Outside reviews are extremely important for products on topics with which the in-house editorial staff are less familiar. Typically, multiple reviewers, with expertise in the areas addressed by the manuscript, are asked to review the manuscript. Reviewers are asked to evaluate the material on the basis of the importance of the topic, clarity, accuracy and validity of the content, value of the contribution to the professional literature, implications for special education, quality of writing, attention to cultural and linguistic equity, and market potential.

If a manuscript or media product has already been developed, the author will be requested to send copies of the material—the number of copies depends on the publisher. The outside review process may take 1 to 3 months. In addition to the field review, a financial analysis is done to estimate the costs of development and production as well as the marketability of the potential product. Also determined at this stage is the proposed format and the projected price that will have to be charged, based on development and production cost.

The recommendations of the reviewers are synthesized by the editorial staff and presented to either an editorial review committee or to the director of publishing. The committee or director then makes a decision to (a) decline the opportunity to publish, (b) request a revision with a stipulation for further peer review, (c) request a revision subject to approval by the editorial staff, or (d) accept the proposed product. Once a decision is made, the author(s) will be notified of the decision and the next steps.

If the proposed material has already been developed, the next phase of the publication process, the development phase, is brief. It quickly goes into a preproduction mode. If the proposal represents an idea for a product that has not yet been developed, the process would take a different route with details negotiated on case-by-case bases.

Development of a Manuscript

This phase of the publication process literally involves the actual development of an initial draft of a manuscript. The timeline for development is determined through discussions with the editor and established in the contract. The time frame for developing a product that is still in the idea stage can vary greatly. Various factors such as marketing campaigns, course adoption deadlines, and conference exhibitions play a factor in setting target dates for the delivery of an initial manuscript.

Generally, a manuscript goes through several stages of revision before it becomes a finished product. Initial reviewers' comments and the staff's editorial judgments shape the product for maximum marketability. Often title, format, and organizational changes are necessary. The editorial staff works closely with authors throughout the revision process.

Ultimately, an initial manuscript is delivered to the publisher and, in effect, this marks the beginning of the preproduction process. The publisher will usually seek another set of reviews of the manuscript. These reviews are then shared with the authors, leading to the development of a final manuscript.

Preproduction activity performed by the editorial staff involves the preparation of the manuscript for the production process. Attention is given to the completeness of the manuscript. A sample checklist of topics that need attention prior to production is provided in Figure 6.2.

Production Process

The production process is typically inaugurated by a "launch" meeting. This is the meeting when the developmental editorial staff hands off the manuscript to the production department. Two major stages are part of the production phase: preprinting activities and printing/binding. A detailed explanation of the production process is illustrated in Figure 6.3. Some variation of this process will be found from publisher to publisher. For simplicity's sake, major components of the production process include:

- Copyediting. Copyeditor reads the manuscript; queries the author(s) about discrepancies, omissions, and clarifications; and prepares the manuscript for typesetting.

- Typesetting. Manuscript is sent to a compositor who prepares the page layout, leading to the generation of page proofs; pages are sent to author(s) for a final look prior to going to printer—only corrections of errors are allowed at this point; revised pages are returned to the compositor.

- Printing. Film is created, plates are developed, and material is printed; initial print runs vary from publisher to publisher; however, an initial run of 1,500 to 2,000 is common for a professional book.

Figure 6.2
Manuscript Checklist

Title _____

Author(s)_____

Dear Author: We need to know the status of all of the components listed below. Please complete this form and return it with your final manuscript.

	Not Applicable	Is this item enclosed? (Please Circle)	
Manuscript			
1. One hard copy	____	Yes	No
2. Disk(s) (ASCII format)	____	Yes	No
Front Matter			
1. Title page	____	Yes	No
2. Detailed Table of Contents	____	Yes	No
3. List of contributors	____	Yes	No
4. Foreword	____	Yes	No
5. Preface and Acknowledgments	____	Yes	No
6. Dedication	____	Yes	No
End Matter			
1. Appendices	____	Yes	No
2. Glossary	____	Yes	No
3. References	____	Yes	No
4. Author biography	____	Yes	No
Permissions			
1. Completed author permission checklist	____	Yes	No
2. Signed permissions	____	Yes	No
Release Forms			
1. Model	____	Yes	No
2. Photographer	____	Yes	No
3. Artist			
Artwork			
1. Figures	____	Yes	No
2. Illustrations	____	Yes	No
3. Photographs	____	Yes	No
Other			
1. Completed product information form	____	Yes	No

Critical Elements to Consider in Choosing a Publisher

Different aspects might be considered when selecting a publisher who you would like to put your product into print. Four elements are particularly important and should be considered closely: contractual arrangements, marketing, editorial support, and production quality of existing products.

Contractual Arrangements

A publisher has accepted your manuscript or product idea, you will enter into a "rights to publish" agreement. This contract will contain many topics to which you and the publisher will agree if you sign the contract. The contractual document should describe many important aspects of the relationship including the following: royalty arrangements, royalty payment schedule,

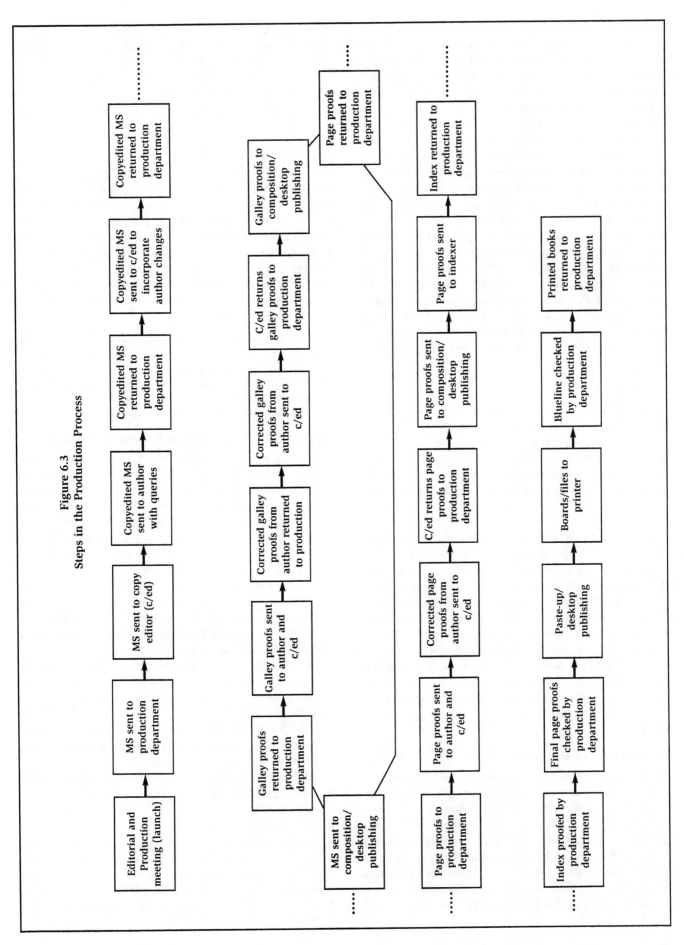

Figure 6.3
Steps in the Production Process

revisions, advertising, out-of-print provisions, termination, death of author, heirs and assignments, waivers and author costs. The contract will also include the date you will deliver the manuscript to the publisher and describe the copyright arrangement. Most agreements have the author agree to not publish any competing works for a period of time. Most contracts will specify what costs the author is responsible for handling, which typically include permissions, artwork, and indexing.

As mentioned above, the amount of a royalty and how it will be paid (e.g., time in a calendar year) is specified. In some cases, the author(s) will not receive any royalties; however, in most cases, royalties on the sale of the product will be paid. Typically, royalties range from 5% to 15% depending on a number of factors. Agreements on how many free copies of the product will be given to the authors and the discount they may apply to future purchases is spelled out. Finally, items related to revising the product and putting it out of print at the end of its useful life are described. It is useful to know that a publishing agreement is negotiable. Publishers use a standard format that can be modified to meet the needs of both writer and publisher. You must not be afraid to ask for changes to the basic contract if you have good reason.

Marketing

In choosing a publisher, you should also think about how your book will be marketed. Publishers who specialize in college texts generally have sales representatives who visit college campuses with samples of their publications. They are eager to provide free examination copies to potential adopters of the text. Publishers who provide products for practitioners are more likely to market their products via direct mail catalogs and special mailings.

Publishers appreciate your help in identifying audiences to whom the product can be marketed. Many publishers will request that you complete a marketing or product information form to assist with the generation of catalog copy and other advertisements. Endorsements, testimonials, and reviews that you can secure are useful for promotional purposes. If you provide training or would be in situations where your product could be promoted and sold, you should also share that information with your publisher. The mention of your product in a session at a professional conference, as it applies to the topic being discussed, is fine; however, the hawking or ostentatious promotion of one's commercially available product at such a meeting is inappropriate.

Editorial Support and Expertise

Another key factor to consider in selecting a publisher relates to the editorial staff with whom you will work. Many seasoned authors need very little assistance in the development of their manuscripts. However, most first-time authors find editorial assistance to be extremely valuable. The support dimension implies that members of the editorial staff are available for addressing various questions that arise. It also suggests that the various aspects of the development and production process are handled in an efficient and organized fashion (See Tip 6.5).

Editorial expertise refers to the knowledge base that the editorial staff brings to the development process. You want to deal with editors who know the discipline and the audiences for whom your product is appropriate. You also want to work with editorial staffs that are author-friendly—that is, they convey to you a sense of sincerity, interest, and enthusiasm in what you are doing.

Quality of Existing Products

No better way to project how your product might look in print exists than to examine other products that a publisher has produced. Although new ideas are always possible due to innovative efforts or a change of personnel (e.g., art director), you can detect a feel for the production features of products (e.g., organization, format, and cover design) by getting your hands on existing products. This suggestion also has value for acquiring ideas about how you might want your product to look. Some authors have identified a type of cover design or a format idea from looking at other products.

> *Tip 6.5: You must continue to cooperate with the publisher throughout the production process of your work.* Be open, but be realistic! Remember this is a collaborative agreement between professionals.

Special Education Topics of Interest to Publishers

Companies who publish in the area of special education have distinct topical areas of interest, as represented by the sections of their print or online catalogs. Unless a publisher has determined to discontinue the expansion of a particular product line, a potential author should assume that new publications are possible for any of these promoted areas. As suggested, one will quickly find out if this is not the case by contacting the publisher prior to submitting a prospectus.

The following topics represent areas that will guide product selection and professional development activities over the next few years, as compiled from various sources such as CEC. Topics of interest, which are listed below alphabetically and which cut across disability areas, include

- Administrative/Legal/Advocacy/Procedural Safeguards/Funding.
- Autism/Asperger/Pervasive Developmental Disorders.
- Behavior Disorders.
- Collaboration with Other Service Providers.
- Cultural and Linguistic Diversity/Disproportionate Representation.
- Curriculum/Instruction/Regular Class Adaptations.
- Discipline/Behavior Management.
- Dyslexia/Reading Problems.
- Early Intervention/Early Childhood.
- Family Involvement.
- Gifted/Twice Exceptional.
- Inclusive Schools and Classrooms.
- Individualized Education Program (IEP).
- Instructionally Relevant Student Assessment.
- Professional Standards/Careers.

- Reading Instruction/Phonological Processing.
- Standard and State/District Performance Assessment.
- Technology.
- Transition/Life Skills.
- Traumatic Brain Injury.
- Universal Design.

Potential authors are not restricted to developing products in these areas; however, these areas have been targeted by various publishers as topics for expansion.

Final Thoughts

This final section provides an opportunity to underscore certain important points and to raise a few issues not covered previously. The list represents a combination of general guidelines and insider tips.

- Never feel that your idea is not worthy of consideration. If you have a good idea and you think it should be in print, give it a go.
- You DO NOT have to have a doctorate to get published. Some of the most practical ideas come from teachers and other practitioners who do not have doctorates.
- "Shotgun" submissions (i.e., sending a prospectus out to every publisher in the English-speaking world) have very limited value.

- Recognize that some publishers have different guidelines for developing a book, material, multimedia, or test prospectus.
- The term *editor* can refer to different types of personnel within a publishing company. Here's a list of the different types of editors: acquisition editor, developmental editor, production editor, and copyeditor. Follow closely the organizational structure of a publisher's guidelines for developing a prospectus.
- Dissertations rarely make for commercially-viable products, unless they are reworked to be attractive to potential consumers in the field.
- Professional publishers are not in the business of looking at your manuscript or looking at your idea for a product, rejecting it, stealing the idea, and then finding someone else to write it. It is a logical fear but one that a potential author has to reconcile, as a publisher has to see your material or understand your proposed idea.
- Worthy publishers will try to recommend other companies to approach with your idea or manuscript, if at all possible.

References

American Psychological Association (1994). *Publication manual of the American Psychological Association* (4th Ed.). Washington, DC: Author

Israel, D. (1987). *Unbound: A spiritual guide to mastery of the material world.* Reston, VA: Entity Press.

Chapter 7
Becoming a Successful Grant Proposal Writer

Teresa Mehring and John O. Schwenn

Getting a grant depends on a written proposal, and the quality of the proposal and how it is presented is a critical factor in obtaining a grant.

—Robert Lefferts

So you want to obtain funds to do something important? One method is to secure funds from external sources—this means a source must be identified and a proposal written. Two external sources of funding are private and governmental; each requires different strategies. In all cases, you must search for funding sources and represent your ideas in a carefully crafted proposal.

Finding Funding Sources

Before writing a proposal to secure external funding, it is necessary to assess your needs and prioritize them (See Tip 7.1). You have to stay focused and clear about what you want, or you will be unable to identify appropriate sources. You must have a solid plan for what you hope to accomplish. Once you have developed your need for funding, it is time to search for potential funding sources. This can be a daunting task! A detailed search is a must to determine the best funding source for a particular project. You must understand the funding source and how it works. Private sources are usually foundations or corporations; and governmental sources are federal, state, and local agencies. Each offers different opportunities so you must match your needs and priorities to the needs and priorities of the funding source (Bounds, 1997). Each also has differing rules and procedures that must be followed to develop a proposal.

Today, the Internet and World Wide Web are two of the most important sources for locating potential funding. Nearly every foundation, corporation, and governmental agency has a Web page that links to funding possibilities and many give good tips on securing funding from their organization. If you do not know the Web address of the particular organization, do a Web search. A sample of potential sites include The Foundation Center, the Federal Register, the Catalog of Federal and Domestic Assistance, and the Grantsmanship Center. Some do have a subscription service while others offer free information.

Federal grants are available from many divisions including the U.S. Department of Education, the National Science Foundation, Health and Human Services, the National Endowment for the Arts, and the National Endowment for Humanities, plus many more. On a daily basis the Federal Register reports details about possible grants and federal activities. Information provided includes a summary of the project, eligibility, funding amounts, and the name, address, telephone number, and e-mail address of the contact person (Knupp, 1993).

Grant information is consistently provided in weekly or monthly newsletters such as *Education Grants Alert, Federal Grants and Contracts Weekly, Federal Assistance Monitor,* and *Education Funding News.* Most provide proposal writing tips that can be extremely helpful. Subscriptions may be expensive but well worth the cost if a proposal is funded. Private foundation funding sources are also mentioned in some of the newsletters. *The Foundation Directory* provides a listing of foundations from across the country (Knupp, 1993).

Most university sponsored program offices have excellent links to funding agencies. University, public, and governmental libraries frequently have resources available in books and pamphlets. Numerous professional organizations have a grant or governmental affairs person who is responsible for securing proposals and giving out monies. Also, as Bounds (1997) pointed out, local businesses and foundations may provide funds for interesting projects.

Others in your area have written proposals that have been funded. Take some time and read these funded grants to pick up writing tips. In addition, attend grant writing workshops and talk to others who have been successful. Just as using models can be helpful in preparing manuscripts for publication, learning proposal writing skills from successful proposal writers can make the whole process a great deal easier.

> *Tip 7.1: Know your audience.* You must assess your needs and prioritize them before writing a proposal to secure funding (e.g., knowledge of funding agencies). Match your needs to those of the funding agency.

Crafting Proposals

Although proposals are always prepared to meet specific grant or agency criteria, most include eight basic sections: title page, abstract, introduction/problem statement, goals and objectives, methods and procedures, evaluation, personnel, and budget (See Tip 7.2). Each is briefly described below.

Title Page

The project title, project director's name, phone numbers, address, the names of the funding agencies, and any required approval signatures (e.g., President's Office, University Research and Grants Office) and assurances are generally included as part of the title page. This page may also include information verifying the project's tax-exempt status. Government grants typically require summary information for the budget including the amount requested from the funding agency and in-kind contributions from the institution submitting the grant proposal.

Abstract

The abstract may be the most important section included within your grant proposal. It should provide a one-half to full page summary of key components of your entire proposal. It should also paraphrase, in a sentence or two, key literature that supports the need or problem for which you are seeking funding—you should briefly outline what you intend to do to address the need, including methods and procedures, and describe how you will know whether or not your approach was effective and successful. The abstract is probably the first thing that a reviewer will read. It should be clear, concise, and specific. Since this summary may be the only element of your grant that some reviewers will take the time to read (Kiritz & Mundel, 1988), you should make sure this section is well-written, informative, and interesting.

Introduction/Problem Statement

In this section, you will want to clearly define the focus of your proposal. This generally involves providing a brief review of salient literature which indicates that others also believe your focus area represents an important problem. To this end, you should specifically define the problem for your institution or agency, and in narrative form, outline the general plan of action which will be addressed with more specificity in remaining sections of the grant proposal. You should back up your statements/assertions with research and facts (Bounds, 1997). You will want to tell reviewers about your institution or agency—why you are unique, other similar activities in which you have had positive involvement, and why you are well-positioned to be successful with the problem-solving approach to be described in this proposal should funding be granted.

Goals and Objectives

Goals are broad statements that provide the reviewer with a general understanding of what you want to accomplish. Objectives, on the other hand "specifically identify what changes will occur. The objectives should be measurable and performance-based, but may also be based on qualitative, subjective criteria, such as increasing feelings of safety or instilling greater appreciation of art or music. Like the quantitative criteria, the qualitative need to be well defined. Surveys or interviews may be noted as methods of assessing qualitative topics like music appreciation" (Stinson, Rebouche, & Laughead, 1997, p. 2). An example of a goal and related objectives is provided below:

Goal 1: The accomplishments of the project will be disseminated in order to influence and instruct a wider audience.

Objective 1.1   Required written summaries will be prepared for the U.S. Office of Education.

Objective 1.2   Written reports will be provided to the State Board of Education, the Office of the Governor, and the University Research and Grants Office.

Objective 1.3   A summary of program accomplishments will be presented at the annual state Council for Exceptional Children conference and at the annual International Council for Exceptional Children convention.

Methods and Procedures

This component of your grant will provide, in some detail, a description of activities you will conduct to achieve desired results and stated outcomes for your proposal. Most proposals restate the goal and each objective in this section, providing a specific description of activities which will result in the accomplishment of each objective, a description of how accomplishment of the activity (and ultimately the objective and goal) will take place, an indication of who will have responsibility for implementing the activity, and a timeline for when the activity will be conducted. A sample from a methods/procedures section is provided in Figure 1.

Evaluation

"Grant organizations want to ensure that their funds are well spent and get results" (Stinson et al., 1997, p.2). This section describes the procedures for determining how and when significant, measurable change will occur. Evaluations can either be subjective (qualitative) or objective (quantitative) (Kiritz & Mundel, 1988). Qualitative evaluations might include such instruments as surveys, questionnaires, checklists, and interviews. Quantitative evaluations often involve evaluators external to the project and the use of standardized measures. Most proposals will incorporate both types of evaluations. Kiritz (1980) recommended that an evaluation section should use procedures that determine:

1. The extent to which the program has achieved its stated objectives.
2. The extent to which the accomplishment of objectives can be attributed to the program.
3. Whether the program has been conducted in a manner consistent with the plan
4. The relationship of different program activities to the effectiveness of the program (p. 28).

Personnel

Often, grant proposals include a section describing the qualifications of the project director and any other key personnel who will be involved in grant-related activities. While a complete vita or resumes may be included within an appendix, the personnel section provides a paragraph or two description of salient information for each individual. Typical information to summarize: the current position of the individual, including the name of the institution; the role the individual will contribute to the grant-related activities; and any unique fiscal parameters which will be required for the participation of each individual in grant-related activities (e.g., 2 months of summer salary).

Budget

Many proposals will require you to complete a budget form provided as part of the application package. In addition, a budget narrative which details the specific expenditures associated with

Figure 1
Methods/Procedures Sample

Goal 1—ESU and USD 123 will collaboratively conduct peer coaching.

Objectives	Activities	Evaluation/Evidence of Accomplishment	Person(s) Responsible	Timeline
1.1 Design peer coaching	Grant proposal development (3 sessions)	Written grant proposal	Project Director	8/97-11/98
	Appoint staff to Planning Team	Planning Team members designated	Planning Team	8/97-11/98
	Collaborative planning of staff coaching program	Written outline of peer training sessions program	Planning Team	8/97-6/98

the grant request is also usually included within a proposal. Budget categories usually include the following: (a) personnel salary and wages; (b) personnel benefits; (c) travel; (d) equipment, supplies, and materials; (e) project evaluation; (f) contractual (e.g., consultants, subcontracts, and mini-grants); (g) general operating costs (e.g., duplicating, postage, and room rental); and (h) indirect costs. Indirect costs are allowed by some funding agencies to compensate the institution for housing the project if such a project has the potential to place undo burden on institutional resources. Some funding sources do not allow indirect costs; others will specify the percentage allowed. Your institution will want you to seek indirect costs if they are allowed.

For each budget category, you will indicate the amount of funding you are requesting (direct costs) and any contributions the institution or agency for which you work will be contributing (in-kind contributions). The budget you submit with your proposal is a best estimate of actual costs. The dollar amounts listed in each category should be as specific as possible and should be rounded to the nearest dollar amount. You must make sure requests in your budget have a direct relationship with the goals, objectives, activities, and key personnel described in your grant proposal. You should also conform to total budget amounts reflected in requests for proposals or other guidelines provided by funding agencies.

> *Tip 7.2: Focus on the details.* Make sure that in crafting your proposal it includes the important elements of title page, abstract, statement of problem, goals and objectives, methods, evaluation, personnel, and budget. The agencies want to know what they are supposed to fund.

Proposal Writing Tips

A proposal must be well-written or it will not be funded. Following are suggestions that will increase the likelihood yours will receive top scores (See Tip 7.3).

Procedures

To produce successful proposals, the proposer must investigate the sponsors, clarify the purpose of the grant, develop goals and budgets, and include all required elements and supportive data as well as get critical feedback on content and writing. To address the issue of procedures, you must

1. Do your homework before writing your proposal. It is to your advantage to know as much as possible about the funding agency whether it be governmental or a private foundation. Most agencies fund similar types of proposals at approximately the same time each year. If you have missed a recent deadline, begin the preparation for next year immediately. Successful proposals can take months to write.

2. Read Requests for Proposals (RFPs) published by governmental agencies. These documents include deadlines, priorities, and funding amounts as well as other critical information. Proposals must be submitted by the due date or they will not be considered. Foundations may or may not have a due date and usually are not as restrictive.

3. Read and reread the application booklet and know exactly what is requested and expected.

4. Establish a timeline for proposal completion. Once a deadline date is known, a timeline should be constructed for completion of each phase of the proposal writing. It is usually a good idea to be liberal in estimating time to allocate to proposal writing.

5. Establish a proposal-writing team and assign duties according to each writer's expertise. Some responsibilities could include *researchers* who gather information, research, and facts from a variety of sources; *writers* who prepare the rough drafts; *editors* who make the final decisions and do the final writing to create one voice; *budget developers* who address financial matters; *proofreaders* who review all final drafts of every page to correct errors as well as ensure the proposal makes sense; and *timekeepers* who ensure the timeline is followed and the proposal is submitted by published deadlines.

6. Communicate with the grant contact person to discuss components of the proposal. Staff members are paid to answer your questions and can tell you if your project is the type they fund, and, if not, oftentimes may direct you to another more relevant funding source. You should feel free to ask for preferences regarding (a) length, (b) complexity, (c) budget detail, and (d) statistical support. If you are unclear about any item in the guidelines, call the contact person and ask for clarification. If budget limits are not indicated, ask, "We are thinking of requesting x dollars. Is this appropriate?"

7. Follow meticulously proposal guidelines and develop a checklist of criteria and specifications before beginning to write; carefully check each item as you prepare the proposal.

8. Clearly match the project to the sponsor's objectives and priorities.

9. Obtain critical feedback from a number of associates before writing a full-scale proposal.

10. Most government agency RFPs indicate points to be awarded to various components of the proposal. Allocate pages for each segment of the proposal by considering the potential points a reviewer can award each area. Stay within the advised page limits.

11. Write the proposal to include specified segments by sponsors. Ensure each section flows logically from the previous one. And, make sure you include each segment suggested by the sponsor. If six parts are required and you only write five, it is highly unlikely your proposal will be funded.

12. Ask the grant sponsor for a copy of the evaluation form used to evaluate proposals. This will enable you to make sure you have included each item reviewers will be looking for as they compare your work with others.

13. Establish only needs for which you intend to create a solution.

14. Set goals to meet your needs. Several activities should be listed for each goal and these should be tied to the budget. Clear, measurable objectives should be stated and evaluation-based. Reasonable timelines need to be established.

15. Include a narrative explaining why each item is needed when developing the budget. As you write your proposal, make sure you are supporting each item in the budget (e.g., "donated," "requested," and "in-kind" columns should be included).

16. Gather letters of support and other documents early in the process. Many (if not all) funding sources require them.

17. Anticipate possible pitfalls and criticisms and address these directly. The first draft should be written for accuracy, clarity, and sequence.

18. Be thorough and do not assume reviewers know anything beyond what you tell them. Write so an educated person from another area can read and understand your goals, objectives, and plan of action.

19. Be sure CRITICAL associates review your drafts and tell you if something is not clear. Have them look for grammatical errors, logical inconsistencies, unjustified budget items, undefined or confusing terms, unsupported arguments, unfounded assumptions, weak documentation, and ways to improve the overall presentation.

20. To avoid confusion and misunderstanding, write N/A (not applicable) where appropriate. All blanks on federal and state applications MUST BE completed.

21. Proposals often need signatures of specified individuals. Be sure to allow enough time to complete this requirement.

22. Reproduce and send the indicated number of copies.

23. Write a separate proposal if you are seeking money from several funding agencies/foundations.

24. Ask for copies of reviewer's notes and evaluation sheets if the proposal is not funded. You must correct these problems if you apply again.

25. Begin NOW for future funding opportunities, even if they will not be available for a year.

Content

A proposal must demonstrate the perfect match between your needs and the foundation/agency. In addition, evidence of research, staff expertise, and well-developed program models needs to be provided. To address the issue of content, you should

1. Begin the proposal with the most important point you hope to achieve.

2. Indicate why the funding source is the most appropriate agency for the project.

3. Emphasize the benefits of your work and why the project should be funded at this time.

4. Quote enabling legislation, foundation founder's words, and annual reports to demonstrate how your project fits the intent of the grant-providing organization.

5. Stress the innovativeness, timeliness, and significance of your project.

6. Demonstrate knowledge of current related literature; cite recent sources and include them in the reference list.

7. Demonstrate the expertise and capability of those implementing the objectives and the appropriateness of your group to undertake this project.

8. Include your plan for future funding once the project period ends.

9. Write clearly and concisely; eliminate unnecessary verbiage.

10. Do not offend anyone; be careful using gender, ethnicity, and education status references.

11. Explain ALL acronyms and abbreviations.

12. Use bold headings to subdivide proposal and underline to bring attention to words and phrases; use wide margins for reviewers' notes and visual attractiveness; and use a readable font that is not too small.

13. Use models and/or visual symbols to articulate your ideas.

14. Use graphs, charts, and maps to illustrate points whenever possible since they stand out more than continuous narrative.

15. Since most agencies now have page limits, and appendices usually are not counted against that page total, append endorsement letters and other supporting materials (unless directed otherwise).

16. Include a Table of Contents for proposals 10 pages or longer.

> *Tip 7.3: Your proposal must be well-written to receive funding attention.* No "ifs" "ands" or "buts"! Try to be as convincing as possible!

Personal Perspective on Writing Proposals

For many of us writing a proposal to secure external funding is a daunting task. It remains so until one writes a successful proposal that is funded and then he or she is hooked. Writing a proposal is similar to writing a journal article or a chapter for a book. It is not done overnight but takes many days and hours and needs to be completed with a clear perspective.

When we write a proposal, we think of ideas of what we want to accomplish. Sometimes these relate to particular opportunities that come from out of the blue while others are thought about, evolve, and are worked on for many months. We read research and collect related articles. If associates have written successful proposals to this funding source, we read their proposals and talk to them. Each time we write a proposal we call the funding agency and ask numerous questions. Some people write better with a team approach while others do better on their own. It is always nice to have others helping with the work but too large a group usually can be ineffective. We divide tasks according to area of expertise and then give each other feedback. One of us takes the lead and is the editor so the style remains the same throughout and sounds as if it was coming from one voice. We continually edit and rewrite until it is time to secure signatures and put the proposal in the mail.

We believe there are numerous excellent resources available that might be helpful if you are serious about grant writing.

Some useful written information and electronic resources include:

Ashley, W. L. (1991). *Funds for educational equipment: A grant-writing guide.* Akron, OH: The University of Akron.

Brewer, E. W. (1995). *Finding funding: Grant writing and project management from start to finish.* Thousand Oaks, CA: Corwin Press.

Dodson-Pennington, L. S. (1995). *Grants across campus—Grant-writing basics.* Arkansas City, KS: Cowley County Community College.

The Foundation Center. (1995a). *Foundation directory.* New York: Author.

The Foundation Center. (1995b). *Foundation grants to individuals.* New York: Author.

Gothberg, H. M., & Ferrell, E. H. (1993, October). New sources on grants and grant writing. *Reference Services Review, 21,* 17-30.

Rushkin, K. B., & Achilles, C. M. (1995). *Grant writing, fundraising, and partnerships: Strategies that work.* Thousand Oaks, CA: Corwin Press.

Websites include:

A Proposal Writing Short Course—http://fdncenter.org/fundproc/proc.html

Department of Education—http://www.ed.gov

Federal Register—http://www.access.gpo.gov/su_docs/aces/aces140.html

Foundation Center—http://fdncenter.org/

National Endowment for Humanities—http://www.neh.fed.us

National Institutes of Health—http://www.nih.gov

National Science Foundation—http://www.nsf.gov

U. S. Government Agencies—http://www.lib.lsu.edu/gov/fedgov.html

References

Bounds, B. (1997). Grant writing for fun, profit, and survival. *CEC Today, 4,* 12.

Kiritz, N. J. (1980). *Program planning & proposal writing: Expanded version.* Los Angeles, CA: The Grantsmanship Center.

Kiritz, N. J., & Mundel, J. (1988). *Program planning & proposal writing: Introductory version.* Los Angeles, CA: The Grantsmanship Center.

Knupp, R. F. (1993). Six steps to successful grant-writing. *Thrust for Educational Leadership, 22,* 17-21.

Stinson, K., Rebouche, R., & Laughhead, T. (1997). Grants: Everything principals want to know. *Here's How, 15,* 1-4.

Chapter 8

Technology as a Toolkit for Aspiring Writers

Dave L. Edyburn and Kenneth A. Weaver

Science and technology multiply around us. To an increasing extent they dictate the languages in which we speak and think. Either we use those languages, or we remain mute.

—J. G. Ballard

Most adults grew up during a time when the writer's toolkit consisted simply of pen, pencil, and a writing tablet. Nearby, the writer's personal library involved a dictionary, Strunk and White's style book, and perhaps, a thesaurus. Conducting a literature review meant spending hours in the library going between the card catalog and the stacks. Needless to say, times have changed. Anyone with an adequate checkbook balance can purchase a computer and a variety of other technological tools for writing and publishing. While most children are reasonably computer literate, few adult writers have been prepared to take advantage of technology's tools.

In this chapter, we examine the question, "What does an academic author need to know about technology?" We begin by exploring the use of a core set of tools: a word processor, electronic mail (e-mail), and Web browser. We provide three examples of the electronic writer at work to illustrate how technology supports the work of the academic author. Finally, we offer a few concluding thoughts on the ongoing professional development issues involved in the use of technology to enhance the writing of an academic author.

Core Tools

The widespread availability of computers and productivity software affords new opportunities for writers to work more effectively and efficiently than in the past. So, given a new computer with a large empty hard drive, what should be on it? What types of software products support the work of writers? What are the essential tools of the trade for a writer today?

The marketplace's continuing development and renewal of products and the critic's never ending search for the "best" products have caused considerable confusion for consumers interested in learning to use technology to be more effective in their work (See Tip 8.1). Unfortunately, in education, there has been little consideration of tools that might be considered "essential" for our profession. Despite the lack of a common vision about the use of technology to support academic writing, three tools have gained a reputation as essential tools for students and faculty: the word processor, e-mail, and a Web browser.

The Word Processor

Within the writing community, there is little question about the value and importance of the word processor. It is a writer's fundamental tool for generating and editing text. Anyone will do. In our opinion, the best word processor is the one you know how to use and have ready access to. A variety of resources are available to assist in the process of selecting a word processor if you do not already have a personal preference (Bobola, 1996; Borland, 1997; Simpson, 1997; Williams, 1990; 1992).

E-mail

Once you have mastered the word processor, sending electronic mail (e-mail) is simple. Essentially, e-mail involves using a software program that allows a user to type a message on one computer and send it across a network, near or far, to users on other computers. E-mail provides an essential communication link for the academic writer requesting information, sharing thoughts and words of encouragement with friends, or writing collaboratively with a colleague in a distant place. In academic environments you are apt to find any one of a number of products (e.g., Microsoft Exchange, Group Wise, cc:Mail, Eudora, and PINE) that support e-mail. E-mail capability has also been built into commonly used Web browsers (Whitford, 1998).

Web Browser

The Internet "is a vast global network of computers connected to each other....[and] allows an individual user to access and share innumerable information or communication resources" (Rivard, 1997, p. 1). The World Wide Web (a.k.a. the Web) is "one area of the Internet that....includes not only printed matter, but pictures, graphics, and sound as well" (Rivard, 1997, p. 2). A browser is a software product that serves as an interface between your computer and the Web. The most popular browsers are Microsoft's Internet Explorer and Netscape's Navigator; many people also have access to the World Wide Web through a service provider such as America OnLine. A Web browser is not functional on the Internet unless you have a connection to the Web through either a direct hardwired connection or dial-in access via a modem. University faculty and students as well as K-12 teachers usually have a free account that provides direct access to the Web while on campus or via a modem from home. Others may need to purchase service from an Internet Service Provider (ISP) that will allow a certain number of hours per month of free access.

Checking Technology Competencies

Knowing the components of a writer's toolkit and knowing how to use them are two different matters. Training is a critical factor in moving beyond the basics and being able to exploit the power of the tools on your electronic desktop. Tables 8.1, 8 2, and 8.3 illustrate self-evaluation checklists to assess your skills in using a word processor, e-mail, and a Web browser. Take a moment and check your skills. How do your skills measure up with each of the three core tools?

If you are a new user, you may want to use these checklists as a guide in developing your skills. If your skills are in the intermediate or expert range, you should think about using what you know to assist your colleagues. There is an urgent need to become explicit about the knowledge and skills necessary to develop the proficiency to use our core tools in ways that enhance our productivity.

> *Tip 8.1: You must be knowlegeable about the core tools of technology to explore your writing strengths.* Go beyond the word processor; connect yourself to e-mail and the Internet.

At Work: The Writer, Tools, and Tasks

The three core tools we have been discussing are essential to the work of the academic writer because they enhance the creation, storage, retrieval, and manipulation of electronic text. Electronic text is very different from printed text. Text that is captured on paper may be reproduced by copying or distributed by faxing. In contrast, electronic text created in a word processor can be modified in seconds and used over and over. For example, it can be printed, copied and pasted into an e-mail message and sent to a colleague, imported into a desktop publishing program to be made into a handout for class, copied and pasted into a presentation program for use in a lecture or workshop, copied and pasted into a new manuscript, published on a home page, forwarded to an electronic bulletin board for dissemination worldwide, and used over and over again. A working knowledge of a core set of desktop tools enables academic authors to create, manipulate, and distribute information in support of all the common productivity demands they will encounter with greater ease and efficiency than otherwise possible.

To further extend the list of possibilities technology affords the academic writer, we focus on three common tasks (participating in the academic community, locating information, and digital publishing opportunities) and how the writer might use selected technology resources to enhance his or her productivity (See Tip 8.2).

Participating In the Academic Community

Experienced professionals participate in a network within the academic community that informs and inspires their writing. New assistant professors often find it difficult to become connected with this invisible college. In addition to having a mentor guide your development and help you make contacts, we offer three strategies to assist you in participating in the academic community:

1. Join a professional association. Extensive lists of professional associations and links to their web sites are readily available. Education Associations and Organizations
   http://www.ed.gov/EdRes/EdAssoc.html
2. Subscribe to a mailing list on a topic of interest. The following sites track discussion lists, interest groups, e-journals, e-newsletters, Usenet newsgroups, and forums. Locate a list

on a topic of personal interest and start subscribing. Messages posted to the list will be sent to you via e-mail.
The Directory of Scholarly and Professional E-Conferences
   http://www.n2h2.com/KOVACS/
AERA ListServs
   http://aera.net/resource/listserv.html
3. Attend professional conferences. Search for conferences by subject, sponsor, city, state, or date.
ERIC Calendar of Education-Related Conferences
   http://www.aspensys.com/eric/cgi/ccal.cgi

Locating Information

A wealth of information is available to anyone with access to the Web. Writers need to consider the practical considerations associated with conducting research with electronic reference materials. First, searching is interactive and allows users to continually define their interests based on the search results and information located. Second, once the desired information is found, it is very easy to save it so that it becomes a part of an electronic reference resource for subsequent use. Finally, this information is readily available for use at any time during a writing project simply by opening an appropriate file, copying selected text, and pasting it into a working document. Here a few places to start locating information:

1. *Scholarly research sites.* Search these sites when looking for specific information regarding educational research and practice.
Infomine Scholarly Internet Resource Collections
   http://lib-www.ucr.edu/
Internet Accessible Libraries
   http://www.ed.gov/EdRes/EdLibs.html
ERIC Documents Online
   http://edrs.com
CARL Uncover
   http://uncweb.carl.org/
Dissertation Abstracts on the Web
   http://wwwlib.umi.com/dissertations
National Center for Educational Statistics
   http://nces.ed.gov/
State Department of Education Agencies
   http://www.ed.gov/NCES/sites5.html
2. *Ready reference sites.* Look for facts or other general information to assist you in gathering information for your writing.
Writer's Reference Desk
   http://www.inkspot.com/ref/refdesk.html
My Reference Desk
   http://www.refdesk.com/facts.html
My Virtual Reference Desk
   http://www.refdesk.com/outline.html
Research-It!
   http://www.itools.com/research.it/
3. *Style Guides.* The academic writer often puzzles over questions about the correct style. Consult these specialized ready-reference tools to find the answer to your questions.
Web Extension to the American Psychological Association Style (WEAPAS)

Table 8.1
Word Processing: Where Do You Want to Be?

Word Processing Self-Assessment Skill Checklist

Name _____

Name of the Word Processing Program_____

Type of Computer (circle one)   IBM/compatible   Macintosh

Check your skill level prior to this course in the Pre column. At the conclusion of the course, check your skill level in the Post column.

Pre   Post   BASIC SKILLS

Prepare a blank disk for storing word processing files.

Demonstrate how to start your word processor and begin entering text into a new file.

Demonstrate the ability to change fonts, text size, line spacing, and justification.

Demonstrate the ability to delete a character, word, and paragraph.

Demonstrate the ability to insert a character, word, and paragraph.

Demonstrate the ability to move quickly and easily through a document (up/down, -line, -screen, -page, -file).

Demonstrate how to access HELP within the word processor.

Demonstrate the ability to load a file from disk.

Demonstrate the ability to save a file from disk.

Demonstrate the use of the spell checker.

Demonstrate the ability to print a document.

Pre   Post   INTERMEDIATE SKILLS

Demonstrate the ability to use block functions (move, copy, delete).

Demonstrate the ability to change margin and tab settings.

Demonstrate the ability to insert page numbers.

Pre   Post   ADVANCED SKILLS

Demonstrate the use of search and the search and replace functions.

Demonstrate the ability to add lines, boxes, or graphics.

Demonstrate the ability to use the mail merge features.

Demonstrate the ability to import text from other programs.

Demonstrate the ability to format text in columns.

Demonstrate the ability to use foreign language characters.

Table 8.2
E-mail: Where Do You Want to Be?

E-mail Self-Assessment Skill Checklist

Name _____

Name of the E-mail Program _____

Type of Computer (circle one)   IBM/compatible   Macintosh

Check your skill level prior to this course in the Pre column. At the conclusion of the course, check your skill level in the Post column.

Pre	Post	**AWARENESS**

I qualify for a free e-mail account through school or work.
I know how to obtain a subscription for an e-mail account.
I know where/how I could access e-mail at home or work.

Pre	Post	**BASIC SKILLS**

Demonstrate the ability to point and click.
I can locate the e-mail icon on the computer hard drive and initiate the program.
Demonstrate the ability to enter your user name and password
Demonstrate the ability to check for new mail
Demonstrate the ability to respond to a message
Demonstrate the ability to compose and send a new message
Demonstrate the ability to delete a message
Demonstrate the ability to print a message

Pre	Post	**INTERMEDIATE SKILLS**

Demonstrate the ability to send one message to multiple people
Demonstrate the ability to create an entry in the address book
Demonstrate the ability to save a message in a directory
Demonstrate the ability to send an attachment
Demonstrate the ability to open and view an attachment

Pre	Post	**ADVANCED SKILLS**

Demonstrate the ability to customize your mail program
I feel comfortable in teaching others how to use e-mail

Table 8.3
Web Browsing: Where Do You Want to Be?

World Wide Web Self-Assessment Skill Checklist

Name _____

Type of Computer (circle one)   IBM/compatible   Macintosh

Type of Browser (circle one) America Online Microsoft Internet Explorer Netscape Navigator

Check your skill level prior to this course in the Pre column. At the conclusion of the course, check your skill level in the Post column.

Pre	Post	**AWARENESS**

I have heard of the World Wide Web.

I know someone who has "surfed the Web."

I have used a Web browser to "surf the Web."

I know where/how I could access the Web at home or work.

Pre	Post	**BASIC SKILLS**

Demonstrate the ability to point and click.

I can locate Netscape on the computer hard drive and initiate the program.

I know how to recognize a home page.

I know how to enter a www address into Netscape.

Demonstrate the ability to use scroll bars.

I can recognize the visual cues indicating a "link."

Demonstrate the ability to select and access a link.

Demonstrate the ability to use the "Back" button.

Pre	Post	**INTERMEDIATE SKILLS**

Demonstrate the ability to conduct a search on the Web.

I know how to obtain "copies" of selected information using the options for (a) Save As, (b) Mail Document, and (c) Print.

I have started collecting addresses of useful Web sites.

Pre	Post	**ADVANCED SKILLS**

I feel comfortable in teaching others how to navigate the Web.

Demonstrate the ability to create a home page.

Demonstrate the ability to create working links.

Demonstrate the ability to copy selected portions of html code from a page and insert this code into a personal home page. (i.e., graphic, animation, format, etc.).

http://www.beadsland.com/weapas/
Electronic Style: A Guide to Citing Electronic Information
    http://www.uvm.edu/~ncrane/estyles
MLA Style Citations of Electronic Resources
    http://www.cas.usf.edu/english/walker/mla.html
Beyond the MLA Handbook: Documenting Electronic Sources on the Internet
    http://falcon.eku.edu/honors/beyond-mla
Style Guide for Online Hypertext
    http://www.w3.org/hypertext/WWW/Provider/Style/

Digital Publishing Opportunities

Today, academic authors have a variety of alternatives to publishing in traditional print journals. Some of the options include publishing on the Internet in listservs, newsletters, and journals which appear only in electronic formats. Electronic publishing is becoming more popular for several reasons. Rather than waiting to assemble a number of articles into an issue or volume, editors can electronically publish an article as it passes through the review process. The information becomes accessible much faster than when published in print. The audience is far larger as well. Rather than mailed just to subscribers, the articles are available to a worldwide audience. Often, there is no subscription charge to electronic publications because the publishing costs for electronic text require no paper, ink, or other materials and no mailing expense. With the opportunity to use graphics, pictures, animation, and sounds, electronic publishing has a greater diversity of modalities to foster authors' creativity and readers' understanding than print. Finally, it is possible to customize electronic journals so as to send to subscribers only an issue's Table of Contents or only an article's abstract so that their electronic mailboxes are not overloaded with documents. Here's a few tips if you are interested in electronic publishing:

1. *Identify electronic journals.* Visit the following Web sites to locate suitable journals that will support your writing. As you browse, watch for e-journals that might be a suitable publication outlet for your work.

e-journals
    http://www.edoc.com/ejournal/
Scholarly Journals Distributed via the World Wide Web
    http://info.lib.uh.edu/wj/webjour.htm
The Electronic Newstand
    http://www.enews.com

2. *Create your own Web page.* Creating a Web page has never been easier. Indeed, this can be a valuable way to archive your work and provide students and others with access to the information. Many presenters use the Web to provide the visuals to accompany their presentation. Most word processors will now create HTML code to make your documents ready for publishing on the Web. A variety of programs (e.g., Adobe PageMill, Claris HomePage, and Microsoft FrontPage) are available to simplify this task.

Personal correspondence and contributions to a listserv or electronic bulletin board join electronic newsletter and journal articles as opportunities to exercise and strengthen one's writing skills and make scholarly contributions. However, we caution you that electronic publishing might not meet a discipline's definition of scholarship (e.g., peer review and original contribution). For tenure and promotion purposes, you do not want at the present time to have a scholarly portfolio that contain only Internet publications. We suggest consulting with a mentor, your department chair or dean if there are questions about the rigor of an electronic publication. Nevertheless, there are ample opportunities to publish and flourish on the Net, and we recommend that you consider them.

3. *Respond to calls for papers.* Monitor the following site to stay advised of new opportunities.
Events in Academe
    http://chronicle.com
A complete listing of events and deadlines for conference proposals, grant proposals, and calls for papers appearing in *The Chronicle of Higher Education.*

Tip 8.2: Stay literate. Your knowledge of technology can help you participate in the academic community, locate information, and enjoy digital publishing opportunities.

Technology Perspective

Traditional efforts to assist writers in using technology to enhance their work have focused on a single tool: the word processor. While such efforts are not in vain, the writer's electronic toolkit has the potential to be much richer. The strategy emphasized here is one of developing a toolkit. A toolkit is simply a set of products that, once assembled on the hard drive of a computer, work together to support the writer in the process of writing. Rather than focusing simply on single applications of technology (e.g., word processing, desktop publishing, and statistical analysis), the goal is to create synergy among applications on the desktop to exploit the power of electronic text. A word processor, e-mail, and a Web browser should be considered the basic toolkit for all aspiring authors.

We have attempted to operationalize a response to the question of what an academic author needs to know about technology in this chapter. We have provided a glimpse of potential opportunities and benefits. In order to take advantage of technological innovations, continuing effort will be needed to identify appropriate tools and facilitate personalized training development to enable you to make full use of an integrated desktop of electronic tools to support your work. All writers need to make a commitment to ongoing professional development in order to exploit the potential technology can offer. We encourage prospective academic authors to seek out advance strategies for using a technology toolkit to increase effectiveness and efficiency as a writer. Finally, we perceive an urgent need to move beyond individual visions to common visions. Rather than allowing technology integration to remain a do-it-yourself project for any writer interested in the challenge, universities, associations, and other professional groups need to foster dialogue about the essential nature of technology to enhance the work of the academic author with toolkits that have been validated by the academic community.

References

Bobola, D. T. (1996). *The complete idiot's guide to Microsoft Word 97*. Carmel, IN: Que Education and Training.

Borland, R. (1997). *Microsoft Word 97: Complete course: Step by step*. Redmond, WA: Microsoft Press.

Rivard, J. D. (1997). *Quick guide to the Internet for psychology*. Boston: Allyn and Bacon.

Simpson, A. (1997). *Mastering WordPerfect 8*. Alameda, CA: Sybex.

Whitford, F. W. (1998). *Quick guide to the Internet for psychology*. Boston: Allyn and Bacon.

Williams, R. (1990). *The Mac is not a typewriter: A style manual for creating professional-level type on your Macintosh*. Eugene, OR: The International Society for Technology in Education.

Williams, R. (1992). *The PC is not a typewriter: A style manual for creating professional-level type on your personal computer*. Eugene, OR: The International Society for Technology in Education.

Chapter 9

Working with Editors of Research Journals

Martha Thurlow, Bob Algozzine, and Dave L. Edyburn

Remember the waterfront shack with the sign FRESH FISH SOLD HERE. Of course it's fresh, we're on the ocean. Of course it's for sale, we're not giving it away. Of course it's here, otherwise the sign would be someplace else. The final sign: FISH.

—Peggy Noonan

Some editors sure have a way with words. And, they should be viewed as allies in the publication process. Don't be afraid to ask editors questions, even though the answers may not always be what you want to hear. For example, a frequent question for many editors is: "Will this manuscript be published?" The unwelcome answer: "Maybe."

What makes a publishable manuscript? How can you increase your chances of having a manuscript published? What are reviewers looking for in an acceptable manuscript? While answers to these questions vary with the audience (e.g., researchers vs. practitioners), content (e.g., report of original research vs. position paper), and publication source (e.g., research journal vs. practitioner journal), a few general tips can be helpful in putting research on paper and preparing any manuscript for consideration by editors and/or other reviewers.

Evaluating Your Ideas on Paper

In addition to addressing questions about audience, content, and publication source, you should think about a few general things as you critically review your ideas for an article. Many of them are related to each other, and taken broadly, they provide a framework for solving problems and addressing key questions related to the publication process.

What is the central theme of the research? Your first task is to present an organizing idea or theme that provides a logical framework for your research. This central theme should be provided early, clearly illustrated in text, tables, or figures, and should be consistently evident throughout all sections of the manuscript. Other ideas can be presented, but only if they are significantly related to the major theme. The relation of your central theme to other research and associated theory should also be presented consistently throughout the manuscript. If your work is published, it will be part of a line of inquiry in your discipline and you should make this link obvious, explicit, and exemplary.

Is your presentation written with simplicity, clarity, succinctness, and parsimony? A common misconception in technical writing is that complex ideas require complex forms of communication. Too often, professional writing becomes bogged down with technical terms, jargon, and specialized language. Rather than "utilizing prolix representations of Anglo-American phraseology," just "use the English language" to convey what you did in your research. You want the reader to focus on your meaning and not to become distracted by your vocabulary, sentence structure, or ability to use an electronic thesaurus.

Have you established logical consistency across sections? Your task in an article is to make a contribution to the literature. To facilitate this, you should link the need and stated purpose of your study to the present state of knowledge and the specific methods you used to address them. The reader needs to clearly understand where you started, where you went, how you got there, and why taking the journey was worth all the effort.

Have you developed researchable questions and related testable hypotheses? A manuscript typically addresses a relatively narrow portion of a field of study. It typically addresses a specific set of questions and hypotheses that can be tested with empirical data. There is wide variation in the nature of these data (i.e., quantitative and qualitative), but the hallmark of published research is empirical decision-making based on assessments that use tests, observations, or interviews addressing specific questions and hypotheses. Be sure these aspects of your work are clearly evident in anything you write based on them.

Have you provided operational definitions for key variables? The mark of a well-crafted research paper is focused definitions for concepts or variables being investigated. These descriptions should determine the boundaries of inquiry in terms that illustrate parameters addressed or how things were measured or reflected in the concrete steps of your research method. Definitions help you to establish the logical consistency of your work relative to theory and prior research. More important, your operational definitions enable others to easily understand and replicate or extend what you have done. Your definitions (and/or the explication of your research procedures) should be so clear that another researcher can take your article and implement your research even if you are unavailable.

Were technical adequacy concerns addressed? Conducting a research study involves moving from words, ideas, and concepts to concrete procedures and operations. Ideas developed in introductory sections, grounded in previous research and theory, operationally defined, and articulated in specific research questions and hypotheses need to be translated into actions that permit meaningful conclusions to be developed. Scientific concepts, such as adequate sample size, control of extraneous variables, reliability and validity of instruments, and selection of appropriate statistical procedures, must be clearly presented for conclusions and generalizations from your research to be trusted.

Were reasonable controls exercised? A primary aim in scientific inquiry is to identify sources of influence related to questions under investigation. The outcomes of any research effort are bounded by the conditions under which the study was completed. To the maximum extent possible, you want to identify and control the sources of variation that are evident in the dependent variables that you study. A variety of methodological and statistical controls can be used. Your task is to convince the reader that you selected the best controls for the environment in which you were working.

Was the appropriateness of the research design addressed? Your goal is to convince reviewers that you conducted a study that provides the fullest answer possible to your research questions. The best design for a research study should be obvious once the research problem is clearly stated. Yet, this design may need to be adjusted because of practical limits such as cost, time, equipment needs, and methods. The purpose for and nature of these adaptations must be clearly presented and the case for the adopted design convincingly argued.

Writing a Research Article for Researchers

Having planned and executed a convincing study, your next task is representing the work for dissemination to a broad professional audience. Systematically addressing a few key areas of professional writing practice will facilitate the likelihood that your work will be viewed favorably.

The first thing to consider when finalizing your research is an appropriate title. The title should be a short (10 to 12 words) descriptive phrase that informs readers of the content of the study. Names of independent variables, dependent variables, and descriptive statements about participants are often used in constructing titles. It is not necessary to include every variable or any outcomes in the title. Good titles include several key words that help others "see" the problem that the article addresses. A second important part of the publication is the abstract; it should briefly summarize the main areas of the research, including the issue addressed, the subjects and method, and the findings. The remaining content of a research article is usually presented in five sections reflecting introductory material, literature linkages and research questions, methods, results, and discussion. A detailed description of key aspects of each section follows.

Introduction and Literature Review

The first section of a research article should introduce the topic being studied, put the study into a meaningful context, and present the problem being addressed. It provides a 3 to 5 page overview of the need for systematic study and the context in which it will be viewed.

The general history and development of the problem being studied is presented first, followed by a section identifying gaps in the literature that establish a place for continuing study. The rationale for conducting the study is derived from extant literature and clearly links what is known to what was learned in the research. This section can be brief or long depending on the nature and content of the literature that forms the basis for the research. It typically ends with a statement of purpose (one paragraph) that presents the exact questions under investigation.

The key in writing the introductory section is providing an analysis of the relevant literature used to support the need, rationale, and purpose of the research that ends with an indication of the research questions being investigated. This section is easy to describe and difficult to write. The objective is to analyze the literature, not simply report a series of index card summaries of articles or other publications. Evidence that this has been accomplished is provided by the following:

1. Acknowledgment of major, relevant, seminal work supporting the need for the study.
2. Relations between key proponents of related research.
3. Acknowledgment of major schools of thought related to topics being studied.
4. Reviews of articles related to key aspects of the research.
5. Critical analysis (often presented in tables) of articles, including strong points, weak points, technical weaknesses of previous research (e.g., sample size, instrument quality, statistics), alternative explanations for outcomes, and possible improvements that should be evident in future work.
6. Linkages between previous work and the current study (e.g., How does what is known contribute to what was done? How will the current study add to what is known?).
7. Common problems evident in the literature that are addressed in the current study.
8. Tables summarizing the knowledge base in key areas related to the research problem.

The introduction and literature review section is typically 3 to 5 pages in length (See Tip 9.1). It is essential to rely on primary sources (i.e., original articles or books) when preparing it. Secondary sources, like abstracts or reviews in other works, generally do not provide sufficient information for critical analysis that is the hallmark of a good introduction and literature review. Moreover, secondary sources are someone's interpretation of original research, and interpretations may be biased. When reviewing literature, it is helpful to use a consistent form to facilitate subsequent analysis and summary activities. Generally, reviews answer the following questions:

1. What was the purpose of the research and how does it relate to the current study?
2. Who participated in the research and how do they relate to the current study?
3. What was done (procedures, instrumentation, data collection, design, data analysis)?
4. What were the outcomes of the research, and what do they offer the current study?
5. What conclusions did researcher(s) offer, and how do they contribute to current work?
6. What strengths and weaknesses provide direction for the current research?

Method

The purpose of this section of a research article is to provide a description of what was done in the study in sufficient detail to enable others to replicate the work. It is generally the easiest section to prepare because it is grounded in what has been done and less open to interpretation and analysis than any other section. Typically, three subsections are used to describe the research method: Description of participants, description of procedures, and summary of the design and data analysis (See Tip 9.2).

The description of participants is typically 2-3 paragraphs in length. It includes a detailed summary of the demographic characteristics (e.g., age, gender, ethnic group, and experience) of the sample included in the study. The sampling procedure typically is described as well. Special characteristics of comparison groups also should be delimited. The purpose here is to provide sufficient information to enable the reader to know who participated in the study and establish confidence that the sample was representative of the population of interest in the research. Qualitative researchers interested in the study of educational processes typically generalize to three areas: To what is, to what may be, and to what could be. Support for each should be addressed in this section of a qualitative paper to also support representativeness and transferability.

The procedures provide a detailed summary of how the research was conducted. Descriptions of instruments, independent variables, interventions, data collection activities, and dependent variables are typically included. Qualitative research

concerns for comparability should be addressed in this section of the manuscript. Technical adequacy information (e.g., reliability, validity, norms, and scale development methods) should be provided to facilitate analysis and replication of the research. The purpose here is to provide details necessary for the reader to replicate the study. In this part of the article, more information is generally better than less.

The design and data analysis section is a brief summary of the technical and analytical considerations that guided the work. This might include a description of the experimental design used, the statistical procedures used for data reduction, a schematic illustrating analysis procedures, levels of significance, thematic analysis methods, and other outcome analyses.

Results

The purpose of this section of the article is to present the outcomes of data analyses in a nonevaluative fashion. The presentation should reduce the data to a series of meaningful statements reflecting the results of the study and should be clearly linked to the hypotheses, research questions, and overall purpose of the research (See Tip 9.3). The section can be organized with hypotheses followed by specific results or with dependent variables used as organizing units of the analysis. The goal is to provide a systematic summary of the outcomes related to the implied or stated purpose(s) of the research. Tables and figures can be used to support the presentation of results; however, tables and figures are used to supplement the text. Refer to every table and figure in the text and tell the reader what to look for, but it is not necessary or appropriate to discuss every element of the table or figure in the text.

Discussion

The final section includes a review of the purpose and objectives, a review of the key points in the literature review that served as the basis for the research and that highlight its contribution to knowledge, a review of the hypotheses, a summary of the method, highlights of key findings, and a discussion of conclusions and practical implications that have been derived from the work (See Tip 9.4). Relations between current findings and previous research are illustrated in this section. Problems, limitations, and suggestions for future research are also included in some articles.

Considerations for Professional Writing About Qualitative Research

You may be asking whether guidelines for professional writing are the same if you are a qualitative researcher. Since the mid- to late-1970s, qualitative and naturalistic methodologies have gained acceptance, particularly in the social and behavioral sciences. While the distinctions between qualitative and quantitative approaches have been summarized by many authors (e.g., emerging foci vs. hypothesis testing, process vs. outcomes focus, and rich descriptions vs. statistical analyses), we believe the two methodologies represent points on a continuum. And, we believe that guidelines for good writing for quantitative research apply as well to good writing for qualitative research.

Still, writers and journal editors alike have struggled with how to present and review qualitative research. Reviewers have asked for criteria for judging the adequacy of qualitative research. As you might guess, we believe the adequacy of qualitative research should be judged against the same basic criteria as that used to judge quantitative research. In brief, this involves consideration of the following broad questions and concerns:

* Are research questions clear and answerable?
* Are variables under investigation defined clearly enough to guide data collection and is technical adequacy addressed (e.g., reliability of transcribers and coders)?
* Does methodology match the questions under investigation; in other words, are appropriate procedures used and are they likely to answer the questions being asked?
* Are participants clearly described? Are representativeness and generalizability evident?
* Are data adequate to answer research questions?
* Are procedures for analysis of data appropriate and useful in summarizing findings?
* Are results clearly presented with parsimony and are limitations of the research recognized?

Table 9.1 provides a brief comparison of these areas and provides a basis for a set of criteria for use in preparing and/or evaluating a manuscript submitted for publication based on a qualitative study. Widely-accepted standards or guidelines for evaluating the appropriateness of qualitative (or quantitative) research do not exist (Vierra & Pollock, 1992). Goetz and LeCompte (1984) suggest that addressing criteria, such as appropriateness, clarity, comprehensiveness, credibility, and significance of key areas of concern forms the basis for a reasonable approach to evaluating the quality of research (qualitative or quantitative). Table 9-2 provides a checklist for evaluating research reports using these criteria.

While addressing these broad areas of concern is relatively straightforward, there are other challenges that face authors of qualitative research studies. Perhaps the greatest that we see as editors is authors struggling with the length of their manuscripts. By design, qualitative studies are often grounded in extensive, in-depth data. This is often a strength of this type of research; however, it does not mean that the report has to be long. Goals of conciseness and clarity remain the same in qualitative and quantitative research. Furthermore, a goal of reader-friendliness has to be considered. Sometimes, this means that a table of broad findings derived from archives, observations, or interviews or another form of summary must be constructed. Broadly, answering the following question may be helpful in preparing a qualitative (or quantitative) report: Have I/we represented the work that was done fairly and accurately in a form that permits the reader to profit from my/our skills as a qualitative (or quantitative) researcher? Asking a noninvolved colleague to read your manuscript before submitting it to a journal is always a good idea, and may go a long way in providing an answer to this important question.

Personal Perspective

Prospective authors frequently ask questions on writing about research that really are questions about writing in general. How do you get started? How do you know when a manuscript is ready for submission? What do you do when a manuscript is rejected? In responding to these kinds of questions, we usually repeat four basic guidelines: (1) Follow the rules, (2) use a model, (3) get input from others, and (4) do it all again.

Follow the rules. Journals in education typically require that manuscripts follow guidelines set by the American Psychological Association (APA). The fourth edition of the APA Publication Manual (APA, 1994) is now the one to use for preparing articles for most psychological and educational journals. Get familiar with it (or with the specific style manual for the journal that you have targeted for your manuscript). Know the basics and apply them in your efforts to publish your research.

Furthermore, most journals have their own author guidelines that are to be followed in addition to general APA guidelines. For example, articles sumitted to *Exceptional Children* must have a section on Implications for Practice. It is wise for prospective authors to know what these additional expectations are and to follow them. Start out making a good impression!

Use a model. Even when you have a general sense of the format of an article, it is sometimes hard to get going. Here is where a model comes in handy. Find an article on a topic similar to yours, ideally one that has been published in the journal in which you want to publish, then imitate what it does. This does

Table 9.1
Comparison of Criteria for Manuscript Submitted for Qualitative Study

Area of Concern	Qualitative	Quantitative
Research Questions	General, open-ended inquiries reflecting interest in describing situations and/or patterns within them.	Specific, close-ended inquiries reflecting interest in describing variables and/or relations between or among them.
Variables	Definitions of variables are derived from intensive data collection activities.	Operational definitions of variables are derived from literature and linked to data collection activities.
Participants	Targeted individuals or groups or those that emerge during a study that are considered representative of focus or research questions.	Random, purposeful, or convenience samples considered representative of population of interest.
Data Collection	Archives, observations, interviews addressing focus derived from broad, open-ended research questions.	Tests, observations, and interviews assessing key components of operational variables.
Analysis	Logical reduction of information obtained from systematic data collection activities (e.g., deriving topics from raw data, developing categories from topics, and determining patterns from categories as indications of underlying themes).	Statistical reduction of scores obtained from systematic data collection activities (e.g., obtaining means, standard deviations, and other measures as indications of patterns of performance).
Results	Narrative-expository style summaries illustrating outcomes and pointing to conclusions to be derived from analysis.	Narrative-descriptive style summaries and statistical tables illustrating outcomes and pointing to conclusions to be derived. from analysis.

not mean that you follow it exactly, but rather that you follow the sequence of ideas, the level of detail, and so on.

Get input from others. Never submit an article that has not been read by more than one person. If an article is by a single author, then at least one other person should read it. If an article is by several authors, it may not be necessary to have an additional person read it as long as all authors have read carefully and made detailed suggestions. It would still be ideal, however, to have an objective opinion or two before submitting a manuscript for "critical" review that matters.

Manuscript writing always benefits from revision, and that is probably the point underlying this third basic guideline. Generally, even the best writers put their manuscript through several revisions. And, it is best if at least one of these revisions is based on suggestions and input from an objective reader.

Do it all again. It is more common than not that manuscripts are rejected. There are many reasons for rejection. However, nearly every (but not all) manuscript that has been rejected can be revised and submitted to another journal. This should almost always be done.

Perhaps the adage "three strikes and you're out" should be applied here, although even this may be too limiting. Some excellent articles in special education journals are ones that were rejected one or more times before being accepted for publication. The bottom line is "don't give up."

Professional writing is hard work. Many more manuscripts are rejected than are published in most journals. Position papers have a slightly higher rejection rate than articles describing original research. Avoiding a few typical problems identified in manuscripts rejected by field reviewers, associate editors, and editors can go a long way in making the whole process more rewarding writers must:

- Identify sufficient need in literature review or introduction.
- Provide adequate description of participants to warrant generalization.
- Provide adequate description of technical adequacy of dependent data.
- Present results in sufficient detail to warrant confidence and direct strong conclusions.
- Describe outcomes in detail that warrants dissemination.
- Avoid overgeneralization relative to scope of the study.

References

American Psychological Association. (1994). *Publication manual of the American Psychological Association* (4th ed.). Washington, DC: Author.

Goetz, J., & LeCompte, M. (1984). *Ethnography and qualitative design in educational research.* New York: Academic Press.

Vierra, A., & Pollock, J. (1992). *Reading educational research* (2nd ed.). Scottsdale, AZ: Gorsuch Scarisbrick Publishers.

Table 9-2
Checklist for Evaluating Research Reports

Area of Concern	Criteria	Rating low				high
Research Questions	• appropriateness	1	2	3	4	5
	• clarity	1	2	3	4	5
	• comprehensiveness	1	2	3	4	5
	• credibility	1	2	3	4	5
	• significance	1	2	3	4	5
Variables	• appropriateness	1	2	3	4	5
	• clarity	1	2	3	4	5
	• comprehensiveness	1	2	3	4	5
	• credibility	1	2	3	4	5
	• significance	1	2	3	4	5
Participants	• appropriateness	1	2	3	4	5
	• clarity	1	2	3	4	5
	• comprehensiveness	1	2	3	4	5
	• credibility	1	2	3	4	5
	• significance	1	2	3	4	5
Data Collection	• appropriateness	1	2	3	4	5
	• clarity	1	2	3	4	5
	• comprehensiveness	1	2	3	4	5
	• credibility	1	2	3	4	5
	• significance	1	2	3	4	5
Analyses	• appropriateness	1	2	3	4	5
	• clarity	1	2	3	4	5
	• comprehensiveness	1	2	3	4	5
	• credibility	1	2	3	4	5
	• significance	1	2	3	4	5
Results	• appropriateness	1	2	3	4	5
	• clarity	1	2	3	4	5
	• comprehensiveness	1	2	3	4	5
	• credibility	1	2	3	4	5
	• significance	1	2	3	4	5

Chapter 10

Working with Editors of Practice-Oriented Journals

Dave L. Edyburn, Fred Spooner, and Bob Algozzine

*The world can doubtless never be well known by theory: practice is absolutely necessary;
but surely it is of great use to a young man, before he sets out for that country, full of mazes,
windings, and turnings, to have at least a general map of it, made by some experienced traveller.*
—Lord Chesterfield

Finding the proper balance between theory and practice, speculation and application is a valued part of many professional careers. And clearly, there is a place for multiple levels of contribution in the development of knowledge in education. Writing practice-oriented articles requires some changes in approach when compared to preparing a manuscript likely to be accepted in a publication focused more on research.

Editors of practice-oriented journals have similar responsibilities to editors of research-oriented journals. Both sets of professionals perform similar duties. Assembling editorial boards, issuing calls for manuscripts, processing submitted manuscripts, sending those submitted manuscripts out for review, making decisions about the publication quality of manuscripts based on the feedback of the reviewers, and corresponding with authors about the disposition of their submitted work are all part of an editor's work. On the other hand, there are some salient differences between practice-oriented journals and research-oriented journals that provide opportunities for editors to exercise diverse decision-making models. As illustrated in Table 10.1, key distinctions are reflected in the overall focus of manuscripts and the specific sections within them.

The overall focus of practice-oriented journals is, and should be, on practical application. A journal dedicated to enlightening practitioners (e.g., teachers, therapists, and other direct-line per-

---

Table 10.1
Key Components of Practice- and Research-Oriented Manuscripts

	Practice-Oriented	**Research-Oriented**
Overall Focus	Presentation of procedures, methods, strategies,or programs for use in building success in classrooms and other applied settings.	Presentation of methods, outcomes, and discussions of original research.
Background	Need and what is known about practice in a given topical area.	Prior research and conceptual literature illustrating what is known about given topical area to establish need for study.
Format	No standard format is used; typically, introduction is followed by appropriate sections of the presentation, including a reference section.	An accepted research format is used, including an opening section introducing problem followed by method (subjects, setting, procedures, materials, reliability), results, discussion, and references, tables, and figures.
Outcomes	Typical comments focus on the ease of appying the procedure, caveats about implementation, and any data that may have been formally or anecdotally collected as evidence of effectiveness.	Typical presentation of results of experimental investigation which may include tables and figures further illustrating findings.
Discussion	• Appears at the end of manuscript, but not in a formal section. • Relates current to previous practice. • May describe problems with implementation or application and suggest modifications for future practices.	• Appears in formal section of manuscript. • Relates current study to previous literature. • Addresses problem areas in the investigation and suggests considerations on future research.

sonnel) will typically focus on translations of research into practice and illustrations of how to implement a teaching procedure as opposed to the specifics of how a particular experimental manipulation was performed and the outcomes of it. Specific sections of the manuscript further illustrate differences in focus. For example, introductory material uses what is known about teaching or practical solutions to instructional problems as context for the overall presentation rather than a typical research-oriented review of literature. Similarly, where standard formats are used for presenting methods and results in a report of research, practice-oriented articles focus more on presentations that enhance replication and encourage application. Finally, articles written for practitioners "discuss" advantages and disadvantages rather than implications for future research, limitations, or conclusions drawn from outcomes and findings.

Writing in Practice-Oriented Journals

Given that any publication cannot accept everything it receives, the editor serves an important gate-keeping function. As a result, it is important that you know about working with editors to increase the likelihood of having your work published. In this chapter, we share our thoughts on ways that authors and editors can effectively work together. From an editor's perspective,

what do authors need to know? We offer our advice regarding five common concerns: Appropriateness, guidelines, focus, review process, and bumps.

Is the Journal Appropriate for my Manuscript?

Deciding where to submit a manuscript for potential publication is a critical decision and thus warrants some investigative work. We suggest that you review an entire volume year of the journal and carefully look at the topics and format of articles. Locate and compare the statement of purpose or editorial policy (see Table 10.2) for several journals to determine the stated focus of each and the types of manuscripts they solicit. Also, search for the author guidelines and whether an editorial calendar has been published describing deadlines for special theme issues that are planned (See Tip 10.1). A thorough review of these documents will provide the necessary information to determine whether a journal is an appropriate outlet for publishing your work.

Often authors have a specific question about author guidelines or the appropriateness of a manuscript for a special theme issue. In these cases, authors may want to initiate a "presubmission inquiry" with an editor. These inquiries, either by phone, e-mail, or in person at a conference, allow the author to ask a

---

Table 10.2
Examples of Editorial Purpose and Policy Statements

Practice-Oriented Journals

TEACHING Exceptional Children is specifically for teachers of children with disabilities and children who are gifted. Articles that deal with practical methods and materials for classroom use are featured. While not research-oriented, this journal welcomes those data-based descriptions that specify techniques, equipment, and procedures for teacher application with students with exceptionalities.

The Reading Teacher is focused on the teaching of reading and suggests that articles should be written as essays and reports of different types on reading and literacy education. Additionally, the journal publishes shorter manuscripts on Classroom Ideas, Literacy Stories, Our Own Stories, Through Children's Eyes, Poetry, Literacy Graphics, and Letters to the Editors.

Intervention in School and Clinic is a journal that deals exclusively with the day-to-day aspects of special and remedial education. Articles appropriate for submission should provide professionals working in these areas with practical and useful information. Appropriate topics include, but are not limited to, assessment procedures, curriculum, instructional practices, and school and family management of the student experiencing learning and behavior problems.

Preventing School Failure is the journal for educators and parents seeking strategies for promoting the success of students with learning and behavior problems. The journal welcomes articles that present programs and practices that help students with special educational needs.

Research-Oriented Journals

Exceptional Children publishes original research on the education and development of exceptional infants, toddlers, children, and youth, and articles on professional issues of concern to special educators. The journal welcomes manuscripts reflecting qualitative and quantitative methodologies using group or single-subject research designs. Articles appropriate for publication include data-based research, data-based position papers, research integration papers, and systematic analyses of policy and practice.

The American Educational Research Journal has as its purpose to carry original empirical and theoretical studies and analyses in education. The editors seek to publish articles from a wide variety of academic disciplines and substantive fields; they are looking for clear and significant contributions to understanding and/or improvement of educational processes and outcomes.

series of questions while exploring a wide-range of issues to determine the "goodness of fit" between the type of manuscript she or he will prepare and the types of manuscripts the editor seeks to publish. Check the latest issue of the journal to obtain up-to-date information about the current editor.

Submitting your manuscript to a journal is the first step in a relationship-building process between authors and editors. The time invested in determining whether a journal is an appropriate outlet for publishing one's work will pay dividends in the form of thoughtful reviews and timely feedback.

> *Tip 10.1: Make sure the journal is appropriate for your manuscript.* Search for author guidelines and special theme issues of the journal.

Are There Guidelines I Should Follow in Preparing my Manuscript?

Most educational journals use the style manual of the American Psychological Association (APA, 1994) as the authoritative source of guidelines on preparing manuscripts for publication. However, many journals also prepare additional information to assist prospective authors. Obtain a copy of the author guidelines for the journal you plan to submit your manuscript to and familiarize yourself with the requirements. It is often helpful to create a checklist for yourself to be sure that you have included everything expected for a particular journal (see Table 10.3). Experienced authors ensure that their manuscript arrives at the editor's office on time for a deadline and with all the necessary information included (See Tip 10.2). It is usually a good idea to contact the journal after 3 to 6 months if you haven't received notice of the status of your manuscript.

> *Tip 10.2: Familiarize yourself with author guidelines.* Make sure your work arrives at the editor's desk on time.

Does Focus Change with Audience?

Articles written for special education and related services professionals typically focus on improving some aspect of current practice. As a result, authors need to consider several factors when preparing a manuscript that will contribute to the inservice education of practitioners and provide essential information for practice improvement: the intended audience and characteristics of their professional life, change strategies that foster practice improvement, and design standards for communicating information effectively (See Tip 10.3).

Audience. A variety of job titles describe the array of practitioners who work with children and youth with disabilities or who are gifted: special education teachers, general education teachers, consultants, school psychologists, diagnosticians, speech therapists, physical therapists, occupational therapists, paraprofessionals, and administrators. More than ever, their work is collaborative. As a result, authors need to provide insight on the collaborative implementation of a practice improvement strategy.

It is difficult to make assumptions about the skill level and interest of an international audience in a given topic. However,

---

Table 10.3
Sample Submission Checklist

Have you

- Prepared a cover letter?

- Provided assurances that the manuscript is an original work that has not been previously published and that the manuscript is not being considered concurrently in whole or substantial part by another publisher?

- Included the name, address, phone number, fax number, and e-mail address (if available) of each author and indicated an address for all correspondence?

- Included a title page?

- Included the manuscript title; author(s) names, title, and affiliation; and running head on the title page?

- Included an abstract of not more than 150 words?

- Eliminated author identification information from all pages of the manuscript except the title page?

- Assembled four copies of the complete manuscript?

- Retained a copy of the manuscript for your files?

- Included a 3.5" disk of the manuscript?

- Labeled the disk with the computer format (IBM/compatible or Macintosh)?

- Indicated the name and version of the program (i.e., WordPerfect 6.1) used to create the file(s)?

- Included on the disk files that contain the manuscript, references, tables, figures, and all information presented in print copies submitted for review?

- Checked a recent issue of the journal to confirm up-to-date information about the editor and submission procedures?

---

it is safe to assume that not everyone is a novice who knows nothing about the topic. As much as possible, target your manuscript at a specific skill level (novice, beginner, advanced beginner, competent, expert) and provide sidebar assistance (e.g., gray boxes and marginal notations) as access points for readers at other levels (i.e., *Resources For Getting Started; Advanced Readings*).

Teachers and other school personnel are more and more facing a variety of constraints and pressures resulting from rapid change, stress, and decreasing amounts of discretionary time. Practically, this means they are finding themselves with little time for reading and reflection. Authors and editors need to identify current issues in the field and assemble information in a form that is interesting, clear, and facilitates implementation. Manuscripts that recite information that is commonly available in textbooks are unlikely to make it through the review process successfully.

Change Strategies. The literature on practice improvement and utilization of research provides a wealth of information on effective change strategies. It is important that authors utilize this knowledge base when framing the problems of practice.

The controlled environment in a research study is substantially different from the typical classroom, and the traditional dichotomy of researcher as producer of knowledge and teacher as consumer of research is a frail change strategy. In contrast, action research and other collaborative roles between teacher and researcher offer significant potential (Ball, 1995; Gersten & Brengleman, 1996; Malouf & Schiller, 1995; Richardson, 1994). Knowing this challenges authors to define an instructional improvement framework and methodology that is "exportable" and one that will produce demonstrable results.

Effective professional development involves a commitment to ongoing learning (Joyce & Showers, 1995). Adults are capable of considerable self-directed learning but need tools to guide their explorations (Candy, 1991). Knowing this challenges authors to create a mechanism for readers to act on their interest in the topic by participating in either organized or self-directed learning experiences.

Learners have different needs at various points in their efforts to adopt and implement innovation (Hord, Rutherford, Huling-Austin, & Hall, 1987). Knowing this challenges authors to describe not only the successful outcomes of a project but to share some of the barriers and roadblocks that were encountered.

Design standards. Given the preceding issues, an editor is challenged to respond by developing design standards for communicating information effectively. For practice-oriented journals, this typically translates to writing style, format, and layout.

Ogawa and Malen (1991) observed that the literature tends to be noninclusive of the views or voices of diverse sets of authors. Using techniques (i.e., sidebars and quote boxes) to enable multiple voices to be heard is a valuable asset in creating articles for dissemination to practicing professionals. Diversity in this context refers to the array of professional roles, race, and ethnicity, as well as viewpoint (i.e., a parent offers her opposition to an inclusion project). Avoiding jargon and "academic prose" in favor of a style of writing that engages the reader also has benefits here.

The hallmark of manuscripts accepted for publication in a practice-oriented journal is a focus on the practical application of knowledge. These manuscripts have a strong central message and communicate valuable supplementary information (i.e., frameworks, guidelines, readings for further study, profiles of the participants and quotes or viewpoints of individuals with a major stake in the intervention described). Issues of format must be addressed by the author in developing the manuscript and are not simply a minor revision of a manuscript rejected by another journal.

With the information explosion of recent years, readers are increasingly pressed for time. As a result, journals are more and more using principles of visual design of information (Wurman, 1989) in layouts that will make it easy for readers to browse and locate information that is informative and immediately useful. Authors must browse these journals for ideas and inspirations about effective visual design formats prior to submission. However, typically, this is a collaborative task between the editors and authors as a revision is prepared.

> *Tip 10.3: You must be aware of your audience, outcome, style, format, and layout when you write, especially when you are writing for practice-oriented journals.* Review recent issues and articles to determine key features of the journal.

What Should an Author Know About the Manuscript Review Process used by a Journal?

When a manuscript arrives at the editor's office, it is assigned a unique identification number that is used for tracking throughout the review and publication process, and relevant information about the manuscript and author are entered into a database. Then the editor screens the manuscript. The purpose of this initial screening is to determine if it is appropriate to consider for peer review. Some of the reasons a manuscript may not be accepted for review involve: (a) The focus of the manuscript is outside the focus of the journal; (b) failure to follow the manuscript guidelines concerning length, format, and style; or (c) if the topic of the manuscript is one on which the journal has already published within the past 2 years or has manuscripts slated for publication on this topic. Occasionally, manuscripts are rejected during the screening process if they are so poorly written that they have little chance of passing the judgment of the reviewers.

If the editor determines the manuscript will be accepted for review, an acknowledgment letter is sent to the author with the manuscript tracking number and information about the expected timelines for the peer review. The editor also selects reviewers who will receive the manuscript without author identification (blind review). Typically, reviewers are asked to prepare a written summary of their remarks and return them in 4 to 6 weeks. Authors are encouraged to contact the editorial offices any time during the review process regarding questions about the status of their manuscript (See Tip 10.4).

> *Tip 10.4: Try to know the manuscript review process to avoid unnecessary confusion.* Feel free to contact the editorial office during the review process.

What Are Some of the Bumps in the Road on the Way to Publication?

When all the reviews are returned, the editor reads the manuscript and reviewers' comments and makes a decision about the manuscript. The options typically involve: reject, revise and resubmit, accept pending revisions, or accept. Only a small percentage of manuscripts are accepted without some level of revision. It may be of little consolation, but less than 20% of the manuscripts submitted to many journals are accepted. Interestingly, many manuscripts rejected by one journal are accepted by another after revision and rewriting guided by the initial review.

Authors who have had their work rejected may wish to contact the editor to schedule a phone conference to discuss the feedback on their work. Authors needing to prepare revisions often find it useful to reflect on the reviewers' comments and make changes they agree with and consult with the editor about comments that are unclear. At this stage, it is important to maintain communication with the editor, especially if unanticipated circumstances arise which prevent you from meeting a deadline. Typically, the editor will again contact the authors concerning the acceptance of the final revisions and clarification of any remaining issues. It is during this phase of the process that the authors and editors communicate most frequently.

The final phase of the publishing process involves activities associated with production of the journal. During this time, the author may be contacted by the editor or production editor concerning copyright releases, camera-ready figures and artwork, and photos to accompany the article. Again, prompt responses to these inquiries are essential in order to sustain established production timelines (See Tip 10.5).

> *Tip 10.5: Know the bumps on the way to publication—reviewed manuscripts might be rejected, accepted pending revisions, or accepted without revisions.* Either way, respond promptly to sustain timelines.

Perspective on Writing for Practice-Oriented Journals

Most editors recall all too vividly their introduction to academic publishing. As a result, we actively pursue strategies to assist new authors in understanding the publication process and navigating it successfully. Readers interested in additional information on the author-editor relationship may wish to consult some of the resources in Table 10.4.

In closing, as we think about what we do, we summarize some of the many ways that authors and editors can work together: We enjoy meeting new authors. We like listening to ideas about work in progress. We are happy to share our perspectives on how a manuscript might be prepared to meet the approval of the reviewers. We are thrilled when a manuscript shows up in our mailbox. We enjoy working with writers on revisions and getting a manuscript in shape for acceptance. We share the writers excitement as each new issue is published. We do not like writing rejection letters.

References

American Psychological Association. (1994). *Publication manual of the American Psychological Association* (4th ed.). Washington, DC: Author.

Ball, D. L. (1995). Blurring the boundaries of research and practice. *Remedial and Special Education, 16,* 354-363.

Table 10.4
Selected Readings for Prospective Authors

Cantor, J. A. (1993). *A guide to academic writing.* Westport, CT: Praeger.

Derricourt, R. (1996). *An author's guide to scholarly publishing.* Princeton, NJ: Princeton University Press.

Fiske, D. W., & Fogg, L. (1990). But the reviewers are making different criticisms of my paper! Diversity and uniqueness in reviewer comments. *American Psychologist, 45,* 591-598.

Garrett, J. E., & McLoughlin, J. A. (1995). A reference for judging the quality of publications in special education and related service journals. *Teacher Education and Special Education, 18,* 133-138.

Henson, K. T. (1995, June). Writing for publication: Messages from editors. *Phi Delta Kappan, 76,* 801-803.

Kupfersmid, J., & Wonderly, D. M. (1994). *An author's guide to publishing better articles in better journals in the behavioral sciences.* Brandon, CT: Clinical Psychology Publishing Co.

Peek, R. P., & Newby, G. B. (1996). *Scholarly publishing: The electronic frontier.* Cambridge, MA: MIT Press.

Candy, P. C. (1991). *Self-direction for lifelong learning: A comprehensive guide to theory and practice.* San Francisco: Jossey-Bass.

Gersten, R., & Brengleman, S. U. (1996). The quest to translate research into classroom practice: The emerging knowledge base. *Remedial and Special Education, 17*(2), 67-74.

Hord, S. M., Rutherford, W. L., Huling-Austin, L., & Hall, G. E. (1987). *Taking charge of change.* Alexandria, VA: ASCD.

Joyce, B., & Showers, B. (1985). *Student achievement through staff development* (2nd ed.). New York: Longman.

Malouf, D. B., & Schiller, E. P. (1995). Practice and research in special education. *Exceptional Children, 61,* 414-424.

Ogawa, R. T., & Malen, B. (1991). Towards rigor in reviews of multivocal literatures: Applying the exploratory case study method. *Review of Educational Research, 61,* 265-286.

Richardson, V. (1994). Conducting research on practice. *Educational Researcher, 23*(5), 5-10.

Wurman, R. S. (1989). *Information anxiety.* New York: Doubleday.

Chapter 11

Professional Development Requires Continuous Improvement

Bob Audette, Bob Algozzine, and Festus E. Obiakor

Once in seven years I burn all my sermons; for it is a shame if I cannot write better sermons now than I did seven years ago.

—*John Wesley*

Continuous review and improvement is a part of the writing process and the rallying cry for important practices driving reform efforts in many areas of American life. W. Edward Deming's Total Quality Management (TQM) philosophy, first used in industry, provides a valuable framework for approaching positive methods of monitoring and change in personal and professional practices. TQM is both a way of thinking and a set of guiding principles for action. Implementing the beliefs creates environments in which groups are viewed as learning organizations with a shared sense of purpose driving efforts toward improved productivity. The principles have had value in transforming failing industries and recently have been applied in efforts to improve education. A foundation of "total quality" thinking is consistency and alignment between purposes of an activity and processes for making it happen. Applying this approach to scholarship as part of professional development means bringing goals of writing and processes for producing written work together. Focusing on the following seven areas provides a practical approach to professional development in writing:

1. Broad goals and missions.
2. Immediate purposes specific to a manuscript.
3. Criteria for meeting manuscript goals.
4. Plans for completing manuscripts.
5. Progress assessment.
6. Evaluation of completed manuscripts.
7. Evaluation of the writing process and progress toward a mission.

Developing Goals

Whether writing represents the totality of a person's career as with a newspaper columnist or is merely one element of a more diverse career such as university teaching, it is valuable to reflect and consider the broad purposes of authorship. Some people write to entertain and sometimes there is a direct relationship between their writings and their earnings. Others write to participate in a discourse on ideas of great importance to them and often increments in income are only indirectly or minimally related to their written products. Regardless of the purpose, it is essential that the author's mission is clear and explicit. Successful writers have clear understandings of what they are trying to accomplish with their written work. Furthermore, they recognize how their written work contributes to their broad goals and mission, and this helps them maintain a focus as professional development progresses.

In the absence of such clarity of purpose and direction, efforts to write are not likely to succeed. It is not unusual for struggling writers to have difficulty articulating the "why" of their writing. This problem occurs frequently when the impetus for "scholarship" is external to the writer as in the case of college course assignments or the production of an unspecified number of publications in efforts to attack the tenure and promotion process within most university systems. The importance of mission (i.e., finding your voice) has been well-articulated in other chapters of this book. It is clearly a meaningful place to start when planning a professional development career guided by "quality" considerations.

Developing Purposes

In the same manner that authors need to be explicit regarding their broad purposes, it is very important that the roles of what they write in the attainment of the mission are also understood. Comprehension of the goals and strategic value of specific manuscripts will enhance the likelihood that the plans for production are adequate and appropriate. There is a direct relationship between the goals of a specific manuscript and the medium in which it will be produced (e.g., technical journal and book), the audience being addressed, the timing of publication, and prewriting work which must be accomplished (e.g., research). Support for making this happen has been provided in several earlier chapters.

Aligning Goals and Purposes

Goals without quality criteria for attainment are relatively useless. For example, if a goal for a manuscript is to introduce a new idea for the consideration of a specific audience, the following criteria might apply:

- Premanuscript knowledge of the audience awareness regarding the idea determines the complexity and comprehensibility of the text.
- Media focus which reaches the preferred audience determines the target or organ for which publication acceptance is sought.
- Media requirements such as length and style must be well understood.
- Desired actions of the audience may require publication prior to a certain date, as is often the case with special or thematic issues of professional journals.

Successful writers identify and monitor their adherence to the criteria for meeting the goals of their manuscripts; suggestions for doing this better were offered in earlier chapters focused on writing in research- and practice-oriented journals.

Planning Manuscripts

The plan for completing specific manuscripts includes
- Identifying the manuscript goals and criteria.

- Considering production processes which have been previously effective for the author and avoiding those which have not worked satisfactorily.
- Establishing production steps consistent with the criteria and past successful processes.
- Setting timetables for completion of production steps.
- Allocating time and resources for completion of work.

Putting any plan into action requires sustained, directed decisions and actions. For most university faculty, this means deciding how to allocate time to competing priorities. It also means spending time writing and revising manuscripts to be submitted for publication.

Using Preferred Processes

Upon completion of the plan, the author implements each step with a continuous eye on the goals and criteria which have been set. The plan for production is useful as a guide toward achieving a writing goal. There is no point in the production process when the author should be unaware of how he or she is doing. If a particular process is not working, the plan can be altered so long as the modifications are designed to achieve the goals and criteria which had previously been set. One method for monitoring progress and quality is to design a matrix with the production steps on one axis and the quality criteria peculiar to that step on the other axis. By checking off work that has been completed, the author has the benefit of a graphic that describes current progress and quality of work. An example illustrating writing steps and quality concerns to be considered in preparing a manuscript on a method for facilitating collaborative teaching in elementary school is presented in Table 11.1. Considering the purpose and goals, audience, and requirements relevant to particular journals as well as matters related to style and pre-submission review are represented. Aspects of each have been described earlier in this book.

Evaluating Products

When the manuscript is complete, it is important for the author to carefully review the work prior to submission for publication. The bases for the review are
- The goals and purposes of the manuscript.
- The criteria for achieving manuscript goals.
- Any additional criteria or considerations which emerged during production of the manuscript.

By practicing this form of evaluation, the author not only enhances the likelihood of achieving manuscript goals, but also reduces and even eliminates the likelihood of a rejection for publishers' technical reasons.

Evaluating Processes and Progress

Unless the author is disinclined to ever write again, it is particularly useful to review the processes for producing the manuscript. Such a review has two important benefits:

Process review provides a reflective opportunity to consider the contribution of the completed manuscript to the broader goals and objectives of the writer. Questions can be addressed regarding the status in achieving the author's mission, the next steps toward achieving that purpose, and even the need for reconsideration of the strategies toward that end.

Process review provides important insights to help the writer be effective in producing subsequent manuscripts. Questions can be addressed such as, "What worked for me in producing this manuscript?" "What did not work effectively?" "What should I do differently next time?" Continuously monitoring professional progress will provide the writer with data to produce more effective production plans over time and to enhance overall writing success.

Perspective

Professional development, including writing and scholarship, is a process that provides many opportunities for performance and continuous improvement. In the first chapter of this book, Obiakor, Algozzine, and Boston noted that there are many reasons to write and all of them are important to professional educators: empowerment, free expression, being on cutting edge (fostering new knowledge), and pursuing intrinsic and extrinsic rewards. They also pointed out that there are many ways to approach writing and all of them are within the reach of all professional educators: Know your story and style, unmask yourself, talk less and write more, and collaborate more.

Algozzine, Spooner, and Bauer (Chapter 2) indicated that professional growth and development needs are among the central themes driving the writing interests of many educators. Integrating writing with other activities (e.g., teaching and service) improves the likelihood of success—this could be particularly intriguing for women and underrepresented groups in higher eduction. They discussed the following suggestions to make the most of writing efforts: Identify a writing style that works for you, think of all writing as a work in progress, use technology to improve your productivity, set goals you can easily achieve, nothing breeds success like success, and build on your accomplishments, don't rest on them.

In Chapter 3, Obiakor and Ford presented additional reasons for writing. First, there are plenty of opportunities to create truths and respond to inaccuracies in the literature and, second, writing provides opportunities for self-determination within a career that are unavailable in other activities. While their discussion centered on concerns of diverse, minority scholars, there are truths for all writers in what they have written: History is a good teacher, but it should not be a preemptor, opportunities for writing and improving written communication skills are everywhere, and negative attitudes do more to control productivity in negative people.

When considering challenges facing novice writers, Goor's (Chapter 4) message was clear: Fear of the unknown and competing priorities make scholarly productivity difficult to achieve. His suggestions for confronting them directly by finding passion, making writing time, pushing past writing blocks, cultivating creativity, dispelling myths, enlisting support, and editing ruthlessly provide positive guidance for becoming happily published.

Chapter 5 (Rueda, Kyles, and Lomotey), Chapter 6 (Boston and Patton), and Chapter 7 (Mehring and Schwenn) illustrate very specific ways to enhance efforts to produce articles,

TABLE 11.1
Example Matrix for Monitoring Writing

Writing Steps/Quality Issues*					
What audience/ organization	Teachers/ Instructor	Teachers/ K-12 Education	Teachers/ Teacher Magazine	Teachers/ *Kappan*	Teachers/Elementary School Journal
Style	Narrative Examples	Step-by-step Examples	Essay Opinion	Descritptive with Data	APA Manual
Target Length	800 Words	1000 Words	5000 Words	2500 Words	No Limit
Submission Timeline	30 days				
Current Time Estimates	hours @ 5 hours per week (one week buffer)				
Assigned Times	Monday – Friday 6:00 –7:00 p.m.				
Required Examples	Need 3 (circle when completed) 1 2 3				

Presubmission Review
  Spelling
  Punctuation
  Grammar
	____
	____
	____
		____
		____
		____
			____
			____
			____
				____
				____
				____
					____
					____
					____

Audience Review
  Pat Jones, 2nd grade
  Morgan Martin, 5th grade
  Sandy Ramone, K-1st grade
	____
	____
	____
		____
		____
		____
			____
			____
			____
				____
				____
				____
					____
					____
					____

*Note: Is goal and purpose clearly established? Prepare manuscript describing method for facilitating collaborative teaching in elementary school.

books and other products, and proposals for submission to funding agencies. These activities are among expectations of university faculty and are the least likely content areas to be mastered in advanced graduate training programs.

To further assist progress from ideas to published products, Edyburn and Weaver (Chapter 8) illustrate the importance of technology and the many ways for writers to use it. Thurlow, Algozzine, and Edyburn (Chapter 9) and Edyburn, Spooner, and Algozzine (Chapter 10) add guidelines (e.g., using models to improve likelihood of success, and varying form and style with audience) for working with editors based on their experiences serving on review boards of research-oriented and practice-oriented journals.

The contents of this book provide a strong foundation of guiding principles for professionals interested in writing. The practical implications of using TQM principles in this process were also presented in this chapter. By implementing quality principles, many authors will find answers to questions they have about professional development activities related to writing. Professionals engaging them find themselves less burdened with unfocused, unproductive writing activities. They also find they have more time to spend with other aspects of professional development (e.g., teaching and service).

Appendix A—Journals Containing Articles About Children with Exceptionalities

The Council for Exceptional Children (CEC) regularly receives more than 200 journals that are scanned for material concerning exceptional children. Articles selected on the basis of established criteria are abstracted and indexed for EXCEPTIONAL CHILD EDUCATION RESOURCES (ECER). Some of these articles are indexed and submitted for announcement in CURRENT INDEX TO JOURNALS IN EDUCATION (CIJE), an Education Resources Information Center (ERIC) publication. Following is a list of journals from which articles were abstracted (current April 1998).

Academic Therapy see Intervention in
  School and Clinic

The Adapted Physical Activity Quarterly
Human Kinetics Publishers, Inc.
1607 N. Market St., Champaign, IL 61825-
5076

American Annals of the Deaf
Gallaudet, KDES, PAS-6
800 Florida Ave., N.E.
Washington, DC 20002

American Journal of Art Therapy
Vermont College of Norwich University
Montpelier, VT 05602

American Journal of Audiology
American Speech-Language-Hearing
  Association
10801 Rockville Pike
Rockville, MD 20852-3279

American Journal of Occupational Therapy
The American Occupational Therapy
  Association
4720 Montgomery Lane
Bethesda, MD 20814-3425

American Journal of Speech-Language
Pathology American Speech-Language-
Hearing Association
Membership Operations Branch
10801 Rockville Pike
Rockville, MD 20852-3279

American Journal on Mental Retardation
444 N. Capitol St., N.W.
Washington, DC 20001-1570

American Rehabilitation
Superintendent of Documents
U.S.G.P.O., Washington, DC 20402

Analysis and Intervention in Developmental
  Disabilities
Pergamon Press, Inc., Maxwell House
Fairview Park, Elmsford, NY 10523
(Incorporated in Research in Developmental
  Disabilities)

Annals of Dyslexia
The Orton Dyslexia Society
Chester Building/Suite 382
8600 LaSalle Rd.
Baltimore, MD 21204-6020

ASHA
American Speech and Hearing Association
  Journal
10801 Rockville Pike
Rockville, MD 20852

Attention Deficit Disorder
CH.A.D.D.
499 NW 70th Ave., Suite 101
Plantation, FL 33317

The Australasian Journal of Gifted Education
Hawker Brownlow Education
1123A Nepean Highway
Highett, Victoria, 3190, Australia

B.C. Journal of Special Education
c/o B.C. Teachers' Federation
100-550 West 6th Avenue
Vancouver, BC V5Z 4P2 Canada

Behavior in Our Schools, see Beyond
Behavior

Behavior Modification
Sage Publications
2111 W. Hillcrest Dr.,
Newbury Park, CA 91320

Behavioral Disorders
Council for Children with Behavior Disorders
Indiana University
2805 E. 10th St.
Bloomington, IN 47401

Beyond Behavior
The Council for Exceptional Children
1920 Association Dr.
Reston, VA 20191-1589

The Braille Monitor
National Federation of the Blind
1800 Johnson St.
Baltimore, MD 21230

British Journal of Special Education
(formerly Special Education Forward Trends)
National Council for Special Education
12 Hollycroft Ave., London NW3 7QL
England

British Journal of Visual Impairment
c/o South Regional Assn. for the Blind
55 Eton Ave.
London NW3, England 3ET

The CAEDHH Journal (Journal of the
  Canadian Association of Educators of the
  Deaf and Hard of Hearing)
University of Alberta, Dept. of Education
Psychology
6-102 Education North
Edmonton, Alberta, T6G 2G5 Canada

Canadian Journal of Occupational Therapy
Carleton Technology and Training Centre
Suite 3400-1125 Colonel By Drive
Ottawa, Ontario, Canada K1S 5R1

Canadian Journal of Special Education
University of British Columbia
2125 Main Hall
Vancouver B.C., Canada V6T 1Z5

Career Development for Exceptional
  Individuals
Division on Career Development and
  Transition
The Council for Exceptional Children
1920 Association Dr.
Reston, VA 20191-1589

CASE in POINT
Council of Administrators of Special
  Education
CEC, CASE Office, 615 16th St., N.W.
Albuquerque, NM 87104

Child Abuse & Neglect, The International
  Journal
Pergamon Press
660 White Plains Road
Tarrytown, NY 10591-5153

Child & Family Behavior Therapy
Haworth Press
149 Fifth Ave.
New York, NY 10010

Child and Youth Care Forum
Human Sciences Press, Inc.
233 Spring St.
New York, NY 10013-1578

Child & Youth Services
The Haworth Press, Inc.
28 E. 22nd St.
New York, NY 10010

Child: Care, Health and Development
Blackwell Scientific Publications, Ltd.
Osney Mead, Oxford OX20EL, England

Child Maltreatment
Sage Publications Inc.
2455 Teller Rd.
Thousand Oaks, CA 91320

Children & Youth Services Review
Pergamon Press, Fairview Park
Elmsford, NY 10523

Children's Health Care
Association for the Care of Children's Health
3615 Wisconsin Ave.,N.W.
Washington, DC 20016

The Clinical Neuropsychologist
SWETS, North America, Inc.
Box 517, Berwyn, PA 19312

Creativity Research Journal
320 S. Stanford St.
La Habra, CA 90631

Developmental Disabilities Bulletin
Developmental Disabilities Centre
6-123d Education North
University of Alberta, Edmonton
Alberta T6G 2G5

Diagnostique
Bulletin of the Council for Educational
  Diagnostic Services
The Council for Exceptional Children
1920 Association Dr.
Reston, VA 20191-1589

Disability & Society
Carfax Publishing Co.
85 Ash Street
Hopkinton, MA 01748

Educating Able Learners
GSI, EAL, PO Box 11388
Ft. Worth, TX 76110-0388

Education and Training in Mental
  Retardation and Developmental Disabilities
Division on Mental Retardation and
  Developmental Disabilities
The Council for Exceptional Children
1920 Association Dr.
Reston, VA 20191-1589

Education and Treatment of Children
Dr. Andrew Reitz, Pressley Ridge School
530 Marshall Ave., Pittsburgh, PA 15214

Education of the Visually Handicapped, see
RE:view

European Journal of Special Needs
  Education
Routledge, Dept. J
International Thomson Publishing Services,
  Ltd.
Cheriton House, North Way
Andover, Hampshire SP10 5BE, England

The Exceptional Child, see International
Journal of Disability, Development, and
  Education

Exceptional Children
The Council for Exceptional Children
1920 Association Dr.
Reston, VA 20191-1589

Exceptionality: A Research Journal,
Lawrence Erlbaum Associates, Inc.
10 Industrial Ave., Mahwah, NJ 07430-2262

Exceptionality Education Canada
846 Education Tower
The University of Calgary
2500 University Dr. N.W.
Calgary, Alberta, Canada T2N 1N4

Focus on Autism and Other Developmental
  Disabilities
Pro-Ed Journals
8700 Shoal Creek Blvd.
Austin, TX 78758-6897

Focus on Exceptional Children
Love Publishing Co.,
1777 S. Bellaire St.,
Denver, CO 80222

Gifted and Talented International
World Council for Gifted and Talented
  Children
Publications Office, Purdue University
1446 LAEB, West Lafayette, IN 47907-1446

Gifted Child Quarterly
National Association of Gifted Children
4175 Lovell Rd., Box 30-Suite. 140
Circle Pines, MN 55014

The Gifted Child Today (GCT)
Prufrock Press
P.O. Box 8813
Waco, TX 76714-8813

Gifted Education International
AB Academic Publishers
PO Box 97
Berkhamsted, Herts HP4 2PX, England

Hearing Loss: The Journal of Self Help for
  Hard of Hearing People
7800 Woodmont Ave., Suite 1200
Bethesda, MD 20814

High Ability Studies
Carfax Publishing Company
975-81 Massachusetts Ave.
Cambridge, MA 02139

ICEC Quarterly
Illinois Council for Exceptional Children
Ming-Gon John Lian
c/o Dept. of SED
Normal, IL 61761

Infant-Toddler Intervention: The
  Transdisciplinary Journal
Singular Publishing Group, Inc.
4284 41st St.
San Diego, CA 92105-1197

Infants and Young Children
Aspen Publishers, Inc.
7201 McKinney Circle
Frederick, MD 21701

Interaction, AAMR
The National Assn. on Intellectual Disability
National Office
GPO Box 647
Canberra Act 2601, Australia

International Journal of Disability,
  Development, and Education
(formerly The Exceptional Child)
Serials Section, Main Library, University of
Queensland
St. Lucia, Brisbane 4067, Australia

International Journal of Rehabilitation
  Research
Chapman & Hall
29 West 35th St.
New York, NY 10001-2291

Intervention in School and Clinic
Pro-Ed Journals
8700 Shoal Creek Blvd.
Austin, TX 78758-6897

Issues in Law and Medicine
PO Box 1586
Terre Haute, IN 47808-1586

The Jewish Special Educator
Board of Jewish Education of Greater
  New York
426 West 58th St.
New York, NY 10019

Journal for the Education of the Gifted
Prufrock Press
100 North 6th St., Suite 400
Waco, TX 76701-2032

Journal of Abnormal Psychology
American Psychological Assn.
1200 17th St., N.W.
Washington, DC 20036

Journal of Applied Behavior Analysis
University of Kansas
Lawrence, KS 66044

Journal of Applied Rehabilitation Counseling
National Rehabilitation Counseling
  Association
1522 K St., N.W.
Washington, DC 20005

Journal of Autism & Childhood
  Schizophrenia (See Journal of Autism &
  Developmental Disorders)

Journal of Autism & Developmental
  Disorders
Plenum Publishing Corp.
227 W. 17th St.
New York, NY 10011

Journal of Child Sexual Abuse
The Haworth Press, Inc.
10 Alice St.
Binghampton, NY 13904-1580

Journal of Children's Communication
  Development
Bulletin of the Division for Children's
  Communication Development
The Council for Exceptional Children
1920 Association Dr.
Reston, VA 20191-1589

Journal of Clinical & Experimental
  Neuropsychology
SWETS North America, Inc.
Box 517
Berwyn, PA 19312

The Journal of Clinical Child Psychology
Lawrence Erlbaum Associates, Inc.
365 Broadway
Hillsdale, NJ 07642

Journal of Communication Disorders
American Elsevier Publishing Co.
52 Vanderbilt Ave.
New York, NY 10014

Journal of Creative Behavior
Creative Education Foundation, Inc.
437 Franklin St., Buffalo, NY 14202

Journal of Deaf Studies and Deaf Education
Oxford University Press
2001 Evans Rd.
Cary, NC 27513

The Journal of Disability Policy Studies
The University of Arkansas Press
Fayetteville, AR 72701

Journal of Early Intervention (formerly
    Journal of the Division for Early
    Childhood)
The Council for Exceptional Children
1920 Association Dr.
Reston, VA 20191-1589

The Journal of Educational and
    Psychological Consultation
Lawrence Erlbaum Associates, Inc.
10 Industrial Ave.
Mahwah, NJ 07430-2262

The Journal of Emotional and Behavioral
    Disorders
PRO-ED Journals
8700 Shoal Creek Blvd.
Austin, TX 78757-6897

The Journal of Emotional and Behavioral
    Problems
National Educational Service
P.O. Box 8
Bloomington, IN 47402

Journal of General Psychology
Heldref Publications
1319 Eighteenth St., N.W.
Washington, DC 20036-1802

Journal of Genetic Psychology
Heldref Publications
1319 Eighteenth St., N.W.
Washington, DC 20036-1802

Journal of Intellectual and Developmental
    Disability
Carfax Publishing Company
875-81 Massachusetts Ave.
Cambridge, MA 02139

Journal of Learning Disabilities
Pro-Ed Journals
8700 Shoal Creek Blvd.
Austin, TX 78757-6987

The Journal of Optometric Vision
    Development
Journal, P.O. Box 855
29 Reckless Place
Red Bank, NJ 07701

Journal of Pediatric Psychology
Plenum Publishing Corp.
227 W. 17th St.
New York, NY 10011

Journal of Psychology
Heldref Publications
1319 Eighteenth St. N.W.
Washington, D.C. 20036-1802

The Journal of Rehabilitation Administration
Rehabilitation Administration, Inc.
P.O. Box 19891
San Diego, CA 92159

Journal of Rehabilitation Outcomes
    Measurement
Aspen Publishers
7201 McKinney Circle
Frederick, MD 21704

The Journal of Secondary Gifted Education
    (JSGE)
Prufrock Press
P.O. Box 8813
Waco, TX 76714-8813

Journal of Special Education
Pro-Ed Journals
5341 Industrial Oaks Blvd.
Austin, TX 78735-8809

Journal of Special Education Technology
Peabody College
Box 328
Vanderbilt University
Nashville, TN 37203

Journal of Speech, Language, and Hearing
    Research
American Speech and Hearing Assn.
10801 Rockville Pike
Rockville, MD 20852

Journal of the Academy of Rehabilitative
    Audiology
Hugo L. Beykirch, Communicative Disorders
Communication Arts Center 229
University of Northern Iowa
Cedar Falls, IA 50614

Journal of the Association for Persons with
    Severe Handicaps (JASH)
(formerly AAESPH Review)
11201 Greenwood Ave. North
Seattle, WA 98133

Journal of the Division for Early Childhood
see The Journal of Early Intervention

Journal of Visual Impairment and Blindness
(formerly New Outlook for the Blind)
11 Penn Plaza, Suite 300
New York, NY 10001

Journal of Vocational Rehabilitation
Elsevier Science Inc., Journal Information
    Center
655 Avenue of the Americas
New York, NY 10010

Language Speech & Hearing Services in
    Schools
American Speech and Hearing Assn.
10801 Rockville Pike
Rockville, MD 20852

Learning Consultant Journal
Association of Learning Consultants
JT Printing & Graphics
602 Mantoloking Rd.
Mantoloking, NJ 08723

Learning Disabilities: A Multidisciplinary
    Journal
Learning Disabilities Association
4156 Library Road
Pittsburgh, PA 15234

Learning Disabilities Research and Practice
Lawrence Erlbaum Associates, Inc.
10 Industrial Ave.
Mahwah, NJ 07430-2262

Learning Disability Quarterly
Council for Learning Disabilities
PO Box 40303
Overland Park, KS 66204

Mental Retardation
1719 Kalorama Rd. N.W.
Washington, DC 20009

Mindscape
Queensland Association for Gifted and
    Talented Children
12 Bayswater Rd.,Milton
Queensland, Australia 4064

National Forum of Special Education
NFSE Journal
1705 Plantation Dr.
Alexandria, LA 71301

Occupational Therapy in Health Care
The Haworth Press, Inc.
28 E. 22nd St.
New York, NY 10010

Occupational Therapy in Mental Health
The Haworth Press
10 Alice St.
Binghamton, NY 13904

Palaestra
Challenge Publications
1948 Riverview Dr.
P.O. Box 508
Macomb, IL 61455

Perspectives in Education and Deafness
(formerly Perspectives for Teachers of the
    Hearing Impaired)
Gallaudet University, Precollege Programs
800 Florida Ave. N.E.
Washington, DC 20002

Physical and Occupational Therapy in
   Pediatrics
The Haworth Press, Inc.
10 Alice St.
Binghamton, NY 13904-1580

Physical Disabilities: Education and
   Related Services (formerly DPH Journal)
Journal of the CEC Division for Physical and
Health Disabilities
The Council for Exceptional Children
1920 Association Dr.
Reston, VA 20191-1589

Physical Therapy
American Physical Therapy Association
1111 N. Fairfax St.
Alexandria, VA 22314-1488

Pointer, See Preventing School Failure

Preventing School Failure
Heldref Publications
1319 Eighteenth St. N.W.
Washington, DC 20036-1802

Reaching Today's Youth
National Education Service
1252 Loesch Rd., P.O. Box 8
Bloomington, IN 47402

Remedial and Special Education (RASE)
Pro-Ed Journals
5341 Industrial Oaks Blvd.
Austin, TX 78735 (Incorporating Exceptional
Education Quarterly, Journal for Special
Educators, and Topics in Learning and
Learning Disabilities)

Research in Developmental Disabilities
(combines Analysis & Intervention in
Developmental Disabilities and Applied
Research in Mental Retardation)
Elsevier Science, Inc.
660 White Plains Rd.
Tarrytown, NY 10591-5153

Residential Treatment for Children and Youth
The Haworth Press, Inc.
75 Griswold St.
Binghamton, NY 13904

RE:view (formerly Education of the Visually
   Handicapped)
Heldref Publications
4000 Albemarle St., N.W.
Washington, DC 20016

Roeper Review
The Roeper School
2190 N. Woodward Ave.
Bloomfield Hills, MI 48303

Slow Learning Child, See Exceptional Child

Special Education: Forward Trends, see
British Journal of Special Education

Special Services in the Schools
The Haworth Press, Inc.
10 Alice St.
Binghamton, NY 13904-1580

Support for Learning
Blackwell Publishers
108 Cowley Rd.
Oxford, OX4 1JS, England

Teacher Education and Special Education
Boyd Printing Company, Inc.
49 Sheridan Ave.
Albany, NY 12201
TEACHING Exceptional Children
1920 Association Dr.
Reston, VA 20191-1589

Topics in Early Childhood Special Education
Pro-Ed Journals
5341 Industrial Oaks Blvd.
Austin, TX 78735

Topics in Language Disorders
Aspen Systems Corporation
16792 Oakmont Ave.
Gaithersburg, MD 20877

Volta Review
3417 Volta Place, N.W.
Washington, DC 20007

Volta Voices
Alexander Graham Bell Association for the
   Deaf Inc.
3417 Volta Place NW
Washington, DC 20007

Young Exceptional Children
Division for Early childhood
Council for Exceptional Children
1444 Wazee Street, Suite 230
Denver, CO 80202

APPENDIX B — Publishers of Special Education Materials

This list reflects the major companies and agencies that publish materials related to children with exceptionalities. The list is not meant to be exhaustive. Publishers not listed here are invited to contact us to be included in any updates that may be published.

Ablex Publishing Company
355 Chestnut Street
Norwood, NJ 07648-2090
201-767-8450

Academic Therapy Publications
20 Commercial Boulevard
Novato, CA 94949-6191
415-883-3314; 800-422-7249

Addison-Wesley Publishing Co.
1 Jacob Way
Redding, MA 01867
617-944-3700; 800-447-2226

Alexander Graham Bell Association for the
Deaf
3417 Volta Place, NW
Washington, DC 20007-2778
202-337-5220

American Association on Mental Retardation
444 North Capitol Street, NW
Washington, DC 20001-1570
202-387-1968; 800-424-3688

American Counseling Association
5999 Stevenson Avenue
Alexandria, VA 22304
703-823-9800; 800-347-6647

American Foundation for the Blind
15 West 16th Street
New York, NY 10011
212-620-2000; 800-232-5463

American Guidance Service
4201 Woodland Rd.
PO Box 99
Circle Pines, MN 55014-1789
800-328-2560

Aspen Publishers
200 Orchard Ridge Drive, Suite 200
Gaithersburg, MD 20878
301-417-7500; 800-638-8437

Attainment Company, Inc.
P.O. Box 930160
Verona, WI 53593-0160
1-800-942-3865

Basil Blackwell, Inc.
238 Main Street, Suite 501
Cambridge, MA 02142
617-225-0430

Brookes Publishing Company
PO Box 10624
Baltimore, MD 21285-0624
301-337-9580; 800-638-3775

Brookline Books
PO Box 1046
Cambridge, MA 02238
617-868-0360; 800-666-2665

Brooks/Cole Publishing Co.
511 Forest Lodge Road
Pacific Grove, CA 93950
800-354-9706

Brunner/Mazel Publishers
19 Union Square West
New York, NY 10003
212-924-3344

Clinical Psychology Publishing Co., Inc.
(CPPC)
4 Conant Square
Brandon, VT 05733
802-247-6871; 800-433-8234

Communication Skill Builders
PO Box 42050
Tucson, AZ 85733
800-866-4446

Corwin Press
2455 Teller Road
Thousand Oaks, CA 91320-2218

Council for Exceptional Children
1920 Association Drive
Reston, VA 20191-1589
888 232-7733

Edmark Associates
P. O. Box 3903
Bellevue, WA 98009
206-746-3900; 800-426-0856

Educational Press
PO Box 32382
Baltimore, MD 21208-8382
410-561-5912

Elsevier North-Holland, Inc.
655 Avenue of the Americas
New York, NY 10010
212-989-5800

Facts on File
460 Park Avenue South
New York, NY 10016-7382
212-683-2244; 800-322-8755

Free Spirit Publishing Company
400 First Avenue, North, Suite 616
Minneapolis, MN 55401
612-338-2068; 800-735-7323

Gallaudet University Press
800 Florida Avenue, NE
Washington, DC 20002-3695
202-651-5488; 800-451-1073

Gardner Press, Inc.
19 Union Square West
New York, NY 10003
212-924-8293

Garland Publishing Company
717 Fifth Avenue, Suite 2500
New York, NY 10022
212-751-7447; 800-627-6273

Gifted Psychology Press
(Formerly OHIO Psychology Press)
PO Box 5057
Scottsdale, AZ 85261
602-368-7862; 602-922-9920

Globe-Fearon
PO Box 2649
Columbus, OH 43216-2649
800-877-4283

Greenwood Press Inc.
88 Post Road West, Box 5007
Westport, CT 06881
203-226-3571; 800-225-5800

Grune & Stratton, Inc.
Harcourt Brace Jovanovich, Inc.
6277 Sea Harbor Drive
Orlando, FL 32821
800-545-2522

Guilford Publications, Inc.
72 Spring Street
New York, NY 1001
212-431-9800; 800-365-7006

Harcourt/Brace
525 B Street
Suite 1900
San Diego, CA 92101-4495

Heinemann Educational Books, Inc.
361 Hanover Street
Portsmouth, NH 03801-3959
603-431-7894; 800-541-2086

Houghton Mifflin
Wayside Road
Burlington, MA 01803
617-272-1500

International Universities Press, Inc.
PO Box 1524
Madison, CT 06443-1524
203-245-4000; 800-835-3187

Jossey-Bass
350 Sansome Street
San Francisco, CA 94104
415-433-1740

Jai Press, Inc.
55 Old Post Road, No. 2
PO Box 1678
Greenwich, CT 06836-1678
203-661-7602

J. Weston Walch
321 Valley Street
PO Box 658
Portland, ME 04104-0658
800-341-6094

John Wiley & Sons, Inc.
605 Third Avenue
New York, NY 10128
212-850-6000; 800-225-5945

Lexington Books
D.C. Heath & Company
125 Spring Street
Lexington, MA 02173
800-235-3565

Little, Brown and Company
Time & Life Building
1271 Avenue of the Americas
New York, NY 10020
212-522-8068; 800-343-9204

Longman Publishing Group
The Longman Building
10 Bank Street
White Plains, NY 10606-1951
914-933-5000; 800-266-8855

Love Publishing Company
4925 East Pacific Place
Denver, CO 80222
303-757-2579

Macmillan Publishing Company
100 Front Street, Box 500
Riverside, NJ 08075-7500
800-257-5755

Marcel Dekker, Inc.
270 Madison Avenue
New York, NY 10016
212-696-9000; 800-228-1160

Mayfield Publishing Company
1240 Villa Street
Mountain View, CA 94041
415-960-3222; 800-433-1279

Mosby-Year Book, Inc.
11830 Westline Industrial Drive
St. Louis, MO 63146
314-872-8370; 800-325-4177

National Association of the Deaf
814 Thayer Avenue
Silver Spring, MD 20910
301-587-6282
Peekan Publications
PO Box 513
Freeport, IL 61032
800-345-7335

Plenum Publishing Corporation
233 Spring Street
New York, NY 10013-1578
212-620-8000; 800-221-9369

PRO-ED Publishers
8700 Shoal Creek Boulevard
Austin, TX 78758-6897
512-451-3246

Prometheus Books
59 John Glenn Drive
Amherst, NY 14228-2197
716-691-0133; 800-421-0351

Research Press
2612 N. Mattis Avenue
Champaign, IL 61821
217-352-3273

Routledge
29 West 35th Street
New York, NY 10001-2291
212-244-3336

Sage Publications, Inc.
2455 Teller Road
Newbury Park, CA 91320
805-499-0721

Singular Publishing Group, Inc.
401 West A Street, Suite 325
San Diego, CA 92101-7904
619-521-8000; 800-521-8545
Sopris West
4093 Specialty Place
Longmont, CO 80504
800-547-6747

Springer-Verlag, NY, Inc.
175 Fifth Avenue
New York, NY 10010
212-460-1500; 800-777-4643

Sycamore Publishing Company
PO Box 133
Sycamore, IL 60178
815-756-5388

T.J. Publishers
817 Silver Spring Avenue
Suite 206
Silver Spring, MD 20910-4617
301-585-4440; 800-999-1168

Taylor & Francis, Inc.
1900 Frost Road, Suite 101
Bristol, PA 19007-1598
215-785-5800; 800-821-8312

Teachers College Press
Teachers College, Columbia University
1234 Amsterdam Avenue
New York, NY 10027
212-678-3929; 800-488-2665

Charles C. Thomas, Publishing
2600 South First Street
Springfield, IL 62794-9265
217-789-8980; 800-258-8980

Woodbine House
6510 Bells Mill road
Behesda, MD 20817
301-897-3570; 800-843-7323

York Press, Inc.
P.O. Box 504
Timonium, MD 21094
410-560-1557